KEVIN KLING'S

Holiday Inn

KEVIN KLING'S

Holiday Inn

BOREALIS
BOOKS

Borealis Books is an imprint of the Minnesota Historical Society Press.
www.borealisbooks.org

Parts of "Ice Fishing" were originally published in "Hook, Line & Television," *Smithsonian*, February 2006.

The Minnesota Historical Society Press is a member of the Association of American University Presses.

Manufactured in the United States of America

10   9   8   7   6   5   4   3   2   1

♾ The paper used in this publication meets the minimum requirements of the American National Standard for Information Sciences—Permanence for Printed Library Materials, ANSI Z39.48–1984.

International Standard Book Number
ISBN-13: 978-0-87351-766-9 (cloth)
ISBN-10: 0-87351-766-0 (cloth)

Library of Congress Cataloging-in-Publication Data

Kling, Kevin, 1957–
    Kevin Kling's Holiday Inn.
        p. cm.
    ISBN-13: 978-0-87351-766-9 (cloth : alk. paper) ˎ
    ISBN-10: 0-87351-766-0 (cloth : alk. paper)
    1. Holidays—Fiction. 2. Short stories, American. I. Title.
    PS3561.L497K48 2009
    813'.54—dc22   2009024483

For Dora Dysart Kling

Contents

KEVIN KLING'S

Holiday Inn

PROLOGUE

WHEN I WAS A KID, after the big holiday meal, my family had just enough strength left to watch television. We especially enjoyed the old black-and-white movies, mostly because those were the only two colors our TV set got. Hardly anyone stayed awake through the whole movie—Dad never made it past the opening credits. My favorite, *Holiday Inn,* featured Bing Crosby and Marjorie Reynolds running a nightclub that was open only on holidays, when Fred Astaire dropped by to dance and make trouble. I loved the idea of a place that housed only holidays.

Another good one was *A Christmas Carol,* starring Alastair Sim. Charles Dickens was right to have ghosts visit Scrooge. The holidays are the time of year for ghosts, unsettled spirits that go bump in our hearts and minds, memories looking for a home. A single phrase can open a door, like an Advent calendar, and out pops a ghost of the past, present, or future. Memories arrive like relatives—some I barely remember, some not at all. *Do you belong to me?* Some enter like a kid pleading, "I'll be relevant, let me stay."

So I knock on the door marked "Christmas Past" . . .

• • •

THERE WAS THE YEAR of the salad dressing, when my sister Laura's new husband, eager to make a good impression on our family, leapt up at Christmas dinner to dress the salad. Unfortunately, he hadn't checked to see if the cap was screwed tight, so while he smiled and shook the bottle, the family watched with horror as Italian salad dressing flew over his shoulder and all over the new curtains.

The year of the peaches happened decades before my birth. During Prohibition, my grandfather had made some of his famous home brew and left it to ferment in the cellar. At Christmas dinner, while the preacher sat at the table, some of the bottles began to explode. Everyone knew the sound and what it was, but my grandfather, without batting an eye, looked at my grandmother and said, "There go your peaches, honey." A catch phrase in our family ever since.

My first memory was the year of the TV dinner. When we went to the grocery store, my brother Steven and I usually sat in the car while Mom shopped. But this year she had lots to buy and it was ten degrees out, so we got to go in, pleading the whole time to go down the cereal aisle for Lucky Charms.

As Mom loaded up the shopping cart, we hung off the opposite sides, stretching out our arms and singing the *Davy Crockett* theme song. Suddenly I got a terrific idea for a science project. "If I jump off, would my brother's weight be sufficient to topple the cart?" The answer was yes. Quite sufficient. He lay in the aisle under the metal cart and all the fixin's, screaming in pain. My mom said, "No, Steven, see? You're fine, and your turkey is fine, see?"

"My turkey?"

"Yes, your turkey. Here."

He carried the frozen turkey the rest of the way to the checkout, hiccup-crying, "My . . . tur . . . key."

Ten days later, when the time came to thaw the turkey, it was nowhere to be found. Who would've taken the turkey? My brother said he had. He figured that if someone broke into the house to steal his turkey, the freezer was the first place they'd look. So he'd kept it under his bed. Now all of a sudden that smell made sense. Also the fact that he'd been sleeping with a loaded bow and arrow in his bed. I kept thinking, any of those nights my father could have popped in to check on us, only to be plugged by an overly protective child. So that was the year of the TV dinners.

Last year was the year of the dog. We have a dachshund named Fafnir. Dachshunds were bred to hunt badgers, which are known to be fierce. I used to feel sorry for the little dachshunds. Now I pity the badger. When you tell Fafnir "No," he hears, "Try another way."

Last Christmas I brought Fafnir to our family gathering. There was food on the dining room table, so I warned everyone: push in your chairs, watch the food, at home we call him a counter terrorist. Then Fafnir made his move. Quick as a flash, he was on the table. The only food available was a bowl of my sister-in-law's famous oatmeal cookies. Fafnir quickly deduced that if he started eating cookies, he might get one or two down before I collared him. So with his face he smashed them all to tiny pieces, then inhaled the entire supply. It was so swift and violent nobody moved.

No one spoke of the incident the rest of the day. I was ashamed. Fafnir seemed pleased. Couldn't have gone better.

The next day, when more family arrived, my brother turned to a cousin, pointed at Fafnir, and said, "See that dog? You wouldn't believe what that dog can do." Then he told the story with the pride usually reserved for an honor student. The rest of my family joined in, adding color and details. They patted him, showing, "See, and I can touch him." Overnight Fafnir had achieved legendary status in a story that would be recounted time and again. I was reminded how Love thrives in audacity. It's why so many girls in high school fall for the wrong guy. It's why a good holiday needs a bit of tragedy.

THIS BOOK IS MY HOLIDAY INN. It includes some of the days on which we celebrate, in good times and bad, what we hold sacred—as people, families, and communities. And now I'll open a few doors, stand aside, and welcome whatever ghosts, blessings, torments, or desires choose to enter.

The Mitten

CHRISTMAS OF MY CHILDHOOD takes place at my Dysart grandparents' home. The house was alive with cousins and dogs. It was a lot of action for my grandmother, so she made a few rules to help ease the chaos. My grandfather's office was a room for work, off-limits to us. We were allowed to enter for one reason: in the lower left-hand side of his rolltop desk, there were books. If we asked permission, we were allowed to go straight to the desk ("Do not touch *anything*") and take out a book.

I moved slowly—this was forbidden territory. The desktop housed a Smith Corona typewriter, the photograph of Granddad receiving an award, a campaign card he mailed when he was running for county treasurer. On the walls were documents of graduations and an odd picture, one that I coveted: "His Station and Four Aces." A group of dogs of various breeds are playing poker, and the bulldog gasps in horror, as he must decide whether to get off the train or play a sure-win hand. I imagined Granddad drawing inspiration from that art.

Then I'm off to his desk drawer, with the three books that would influence my thoughts throughout life. The first, *Curious George Goes to the Hospital,* was about a monkey who swallows a puzzle piece and is rushed to the emergency room. The information in that book got me through many long months of childhood hospital visits. It taught me to survive and stay curious, and it also gave me a life-long desire to get a monkey.

Another was a Little Golden Book called *The Little Engine That Could,* about a small engine that agreed to pull a train over a hill when all the big engines said no. He kept repeating, "I think I can, I think I can" until he got to the top, and then yelled, "I thought I could, I thought I could!" as he raced down the other side. I would think of his example every time I ran a marathon or went on a date.

The third book, a Ukrainian folktale called *The Mitten,* was full of colorful pictures. It's the story of a little boy who loses a mitten. One by one, forest creatures come upon it: a mouse, a frog, a fox, and finally, a bear. Each one crawls into the mitten for warmth, joining the others who came before. Finally, the boy returns and the animals scatter into the forest.

I loved that story. I did wonder how a mitten could hold a bear and a fox—it seemed impossible. But like the boy in the story, I was forever losing mittens. Because my left arm is much shorter than my right, I would simply tuck my arm into my sleeve. Our neighborhood was full of perfectly good left-handed mittens strewn about because I never wore them. I liked to imagine my lost mittens provided housing for all the animals between home and school. I read that book until the paper felt as soft as cloth. Like all good stories, it also had an element to it that I couldn't put my finger on, a deeper level that I didn't understand. But it made me feel good.

ONE YEAR MY PARENTS decide to host Christmas. I'm fifteen years old, waking up in my twin bed. Big Daddy Roth Hot Rods and pictures of major league ball players adorn my room.

In the living room I faintly hear a Texaco Star Theater Christmas album playing, with Johnny Mathis, Nat King Cole, Patsy Cline, Doris Day singing Christmas songs.

Under the tree, boxes and boxes. What could there be? In the past I would wish for Matchbox or Hot Wheels cars, Tonka Trucks, Lincoln Logs, an Etch A Sketch, an Erector Set, hockey skates, a chemistry set, a crystal radio, GI Joes, Rock 'Em Sock 'Em Robots, a Chatty Cathy doll for my sister. Oh, and a piece of coal for my brother.

But I have put aside my childish ways and now hope "Santa" brings me a Visible V8 engine, a model of a real working car engine, oh, and Santa, don't forget the glue this time. Also in my more mature self I wish for a nice dress for my sister. And something for my brother . . . socks.

We unwrap the presents, and I get the Visible V8 and glue. Then we wrap ourselves in coats and scarves and bundle off to church. Inside the church it always smells of hair tonic, perfume, and burning candles, clean bodies and cleansing souls. A list of names is etched on the wall of the sanctuary. When I was little, I asked my mother who they were. She said, "The men who died in the service." I remember wondering if it was the first service or the second service.

The pastor has a habit of flailing a point long past its expiration date. The worst was the Sunday he read through the entire list of "begats" in Genesis.

> And the sons of Ham; Cush, and Mizraim, and Phut, and Canaan. And the sons of Cush; Seba, and Havilah, and Sabtah, and Raamah, and Sabtechah: and the sons of Raamah; Sheba, and Dedan. And Cush begat Nimrod . . . And the beginning of his kingdom was Babel, and Erech, and Accad, and Calneh, in the land of Shinar. Out of that land went forth Asshur, and builded Nineveh, and the city Rehoboth, and Calah, And Resen between Nineveh and Calah: the same is a great city. And Mizraim begat Ludim, and Anamim, and Lehabim, and Naphtuhim, and Pathrusim, and Casluhim (out of whom came Philistim), and Caphtorim.

I've been told there are actors who can read a phone book and make it interesting, but the pastor wasn't one of them. His message was that Jesus was born of a line, as are we all, and one day we, too, will be part of the "begats." I liked his point, especially that maybe I would be associated with my grandpa's strong arms, my grandma's love, my mom's beauty, and my dad's humor.

Luckily, every Christmas we attend the special early service provided by the youth group. In my teen years it features high school kids half-heartedly muddling through some scripture, maybe with a guitar as their weapon of defiance, a rendition of "Michael, Row the Boat Ashore" causing many dads to say, "That does it, what has happened to the sanctity of religion, from now on I'm sleeping in on Sundays." Then the beaming youth pastor gets up to deliver the early service sermon. It's his one big shot. He talks about Jesus "making the scene" at Bethlehem, calls Herod "the man" and says he wore "groovy threads." He reads from his *Good News Bible,* taking a few liberties—the shortest verse becomes "Jesus was bummed." As the youth pastor talks of Egypt, it's pretty obvious he's really talking about Vietnam, but he sticks to the "live by the sword" doctrine. Every once in a while, he glances over to the senior pastor, who lowers his eyebrows and shifts uncomfortably.

One year the combination of films like *Airport* and *The Poseidon Adventure* with the newly popular Moog synthesizer inspires a program entitled "Disasters of the Bible." It is clear from the outset that the youth pastor had no hand in this. Probably out of fear of becoming "the man," he has let the students have their way. He sits to the side and folds his arms, as the head pastor gives him a worried look and folds his arms, as well.

The lights dim. The organist, a woman in her seventies, begins playing a selection from Grieg's *Peer Gynt,* but to me, it's the sunrise music from a Bugs Bunny cartoon. A student reads "The dawn of time" into a microphone.

"In the beginning there was paradise.

"But then came man . . . greed, avarice, lust.

"God provided us with a perfect world, but man couldn't leave well enough alone."

The organist leans into Bach.

"And God sayeth, 'Don't make me come down there.' But did man listen?"

The chorus says, "NO!"

"THEN YE SHALL KNOW MY WRATH!"

A rumbling sound begins. At first, it feels like it's coming from underneath us. Kids look under pews. Not there. The rumbling grows as Bach crescendos. Finally, the synthesizer is used to full effect as we are ushered through catastrophes of Biblical proportions.

The Great Flood:

"Ruth, my hand, take my hand," yells a student.

And another wails, "I can't reach!"

"Ruth . . . nooooo."

Moses in the land of Egypt:

"Pharaoh, let my people go."

"No."

Sonic walls of high-pitched locusts.

"NO."

Sounds of oozing blood.

"Okay, go."

A wall of Red Sea, a bit similar to the Great Flood:

Chorus yells, "Noooooo."

The Towering Inferno of Babel:

"She's gonna blow!"

The walls of Jericho:

The organist is now caught in the moment, hammering the bass line to "Smoke on the Water," her legs and arms flying like a marionette in an earthquake. Then a glowing cradle emerges to "Fanfare for the Common Man."

"A new day dawns. Thank you and amen."

By the end, our ears are bleeding. The farmers, motionless, have frozen looks of terror. The students, clearly pleased, hold hands and bow politely. The skinny farm kid on the synthesizer high-fives the organist. She grins, seems to have waited her whole life for this. The audience—I mean congregation—bursts into applause. Applause, in church.

Both the pastor and youth pastor seem surprised and displeased by the reaction. Christmas is clearly now in the hands of the masses. Not good.

WE ARRIVE HOME just as a 1962 Volkswagen Beetle pulls up in front of our house. It's my mom's sister and her family of five and a Chihuahua. They pile out of this Bug like it's a clown car.

More relatives arrive. One uncle says, "Put 'er in the vise," and gives me a knuckle-busting handshake. The aunts go straight to the kitchen, like something has already gone horribly wrong and they've arrived just in time.

Uncle Don, my dad's brother, asks why we didn't get a full-size tree this year. Dad says he likes this tree fine. His brother comments there are three things in life that can never be too big and leaves it at that. I'm guessing one is a tree.

I learn from Uncle Don that no matter what he has achieved in life, no matter what the world thinks of him, whenever Dad's with my uncle, Don will always be second son from the bottom. I look over at my little brother and smile.

Uncle Johnny goes into the bathroom. He's the uncle who is fun and funny on his farm, but everywhere else he is very nervous and unsure. Even his clothes look like they don't want to be on him. Whenever he comes over to our house, he has to fix something.

Johnny is in the bathroom a long time. When Dad opens the door, he finds Uncle Johnny and a dismantled toilet.

Dad says, "Johnny, what are you doing? Somebody might need that."

Johnny informs Dad the wax ring was going, in fact, was about to blow. He makes a noise like the synthesizer in the flood scene at church. He tells Dad he'll have it fixed in a jiffy, if Dad brings him his spare ring.

Dad says, "A wax ring? Why would I have a wax ring?"

Johnny says, "In case this happens."

Dad says he's fresh out of wax rings, so Johnny asks where the nearest hardware store is.

Dad says they won't be open on Christmas, but Johnny puts on his coat and says he'll be right back.

Now the aunts are going full steam in the kitchen. One on the gravy, one on the potatoes. My mom is sitting out of the way, drinking coffee.

My sister's new husband is in the mix, too, learning secrets no book would dare reveal. He's in heaven and so are they. A man who cooks is as rare as a car that gets over ten miles to the gallon.

In the living room, the uncles are in full swing, as well, arguing Ford versus Chevy, electric shaver versus razor, gas versus charcoal, Tums versus Rolaids, Labs versus spaniels, boxers versus tidy whities.

My uncle tells Dad Ford stands for Found On Road Dead. Dad corrects him: No, he heard First On Race Day.

One uncle drinks from a coffee mug, smiles, and says, "Everything in moderation," but it sounds like he emphasizes the "everything" part.

I love my uncles. They are eccentric but have good hearts, and like all good uncles, they teach me a lot. Usually they show me what not to do by doing it. Like the year Uncle Byron got the midlife perm. (Note to self: don't do that.)

In the kitchen we hear laughter. Aunt Mary has told about Johnny's condition with his circulation. On doctor's orders, she has to tie his hands behind his back. She's worried that tying up her husband six times a day makes her kinky. Mom says not unless she enjoys it, and as everyone laughs, Mary gets a worried look on her face.

Then Johnny comes back in with a wax ring. Says he ran into a guy in the parking lot of the hardware store who was putting a subfloor in his nephew's basement. The guy happened to have a wax ring at his house, so my uncle traded him some rebar that he had in the back of the truck.

The toilet now repaired, and the wax ring dubbed a Christmas miracle, we say grace and dig into dinner.

Even now, I can look around that dining room table at

those faces. My relatives. How, why? We are all so different. Everyone is pretty funny, and it's a good bunch of people, but it's pretty clear that our gene pool doesn't have a deep end.

Mom walks out with a special treat, a country ham.

FOR CHRISTMAS DINNER at my Grandmother Dysart's house, we always had country ham. Country ham is preserved with salt. Pounds of salt, sugar, and pepper. It's tightly packed with the spices, then wrapped in a cloth bag and hung in a ventilated place for months, years. Granddad had a special, seriously off-limits shed for hams out back of the house. A week before Christmas, Granddad would take a ham down from the rafters and cut off the thick mold that now enveloped it. Inside that horrible mass of rotting cloth, mold, and fat is the most delicious, salty treat, like a magic meat geode. Usually the ham is soaked for a day or two before cooking to try to pull some of the salt out. Grandma used 7-Up, but I'm not sure if this makes a noticeable difference. Country ham is not an acquired taste. You have to be born to it. It's like other foods from cultures all around the globe, dishes that used various techniques for preserving food before refrigeration, lutefisk in Norway or sauerkraut in Germany or kimchee in Korea. They are flavors we don't really need any more, but they remind us of how good we've got it. Flavors not for the timid.

At three o'clock the next the morning, I'll wake up and rush to the kitchen for water, where I'll find all my relatives huddled around the sink and a running tap. There isn't even time for a cup. The mouth goes right to the tap. After at least a gallon of water, the two strongmen squeezing my kidneys slowly release, and it's back to bed.

MOM SETS THE HAM DOWN. Somehow she had found a country ham, made in the same county where her parents had lived.

The whole table gasps. It feels like the Cratchits' house on Christmas, when the table of guests is astonished at the turkey. The younger kids are asking, "What is it?"

"You're going to like it."

And they do.

After dinner we assemble in the living room

Warmed with apple cider, we sit in front of the Zenith TV. We watch *The Ten Commandments* in Technicolor. Edward G. Robinson is the slave master and talks like he's smoking a stogie: "Yah, Moses, where is your God now, see?"

Then *It's a Wonderful Life* comes on. My uncles love Mr. Potter, the villain. They explain that a hero is only as good as his nemesis is bad. They love it that Mr. Potter never learns his lesson. They figure if Scrooge had taken NyQuil, he would have got away with everything, too.

I like watching Bambi with my uncles, all avid hunters. By the end of the movie, you're shouting, "There's one—in the meadow."

The aunts move into the living room and we turn off the TV. It's time to visit. We hear about relatives we never knew. These aunts are responsible for our family tree, and they're expert pruners, leaving all branches neatly trimmed.

I often wonder who was lost to their shears. Sometimes their topiary looks good, but it's at the expense of some interesting fruit.

The unmarked present under the tree has been unwrapped, and all the uncles sip from coffee mugs. "Can I have a taste?" An uncle hands me his cup, but an aunt intercedes: "Absolutely not."

An uncle tells about the time he got an orange and a comb during the Great Depression, tears up, and sips from his coffee mug. There's an argument over who got the dog. "I got the dog." "No, that was my dog." "Well, he never minded you." "But he was mine." I look at my brother, and we both realize we're looking at the future.

A cousin reads a Bible verse.

We all remember the Christmases at my grandparents' farm, everyone laughs, and it grows silent for a minute.

A cousin's new baby gets passed around. Even I get to hold her. She smells so good—new baby smell is even better than new car smell. I have to be so careful with her. The future.

As I hold her, it seems clear why God sent Jesus as a baby. When it came time to teach a sinning world a lesson, what else could he send? He'd already tried floods, bugs, famine, and other devastations. What would he visit upon a corrupt and careless world? A baby. Fragile and helpless. Take care of your faith, or it will die.

God was so way ahead of us. It's like when my brother looks at a rock, and my Dad says, "Don't even think about it." How does he know?

The uncles and dad go to the basement with the ice cream maker. They take turns adding the salt and ice and turning the crank that spins the drum. It's a challenge, because the ice and salt jam the works, so it immediately becomes a competition, which uncle can spin the fastest.

We have ice cream and pie. Then an uncle says, "Well, I s'pose," and it's the early warning sign that the visit has ended. The cousins pile back into the clown car and drive off into the night.

I go up to bed and fall asleep hearing my parents' muffled voices as they clean up the house. There is nothing better than falling asleep to that sound. I think again of my grandparents. I think of *The Mitten,* the book in Granddad's drawer. My family is like that mitten. It seems impossible that we could all fit, but we do, we all belong.

And of course I would see them in a couple of hours, at the kitchen sink.

Otto

I WANT TO TELL YOU ABOUT a guy named Otto and the advice he gave me one winter solstice, but first you have to know a little bit about ice fishing.

Every November in Minnesota, the call goes out: "The ice is safe." Open water has turned into prime real estate, and overnight, clusters of tiny shacks pop up on frozen lakes. Ice fishing season has begun in the nation's icebox, Paul Bunyan country, where carpaccio is still made with real carp and an especially frigid winter is referred to by its year, like a fine vintage wine.

Although months of below-zero temperatures test the heartiest souls, surprisingly, a good number of people live here on purpose. I overheard one northern gentleman say, "When you freeze paradise, it's bound to last a little longer." It's true, however, that one must either get out and embrace the winter or suffer the consequences of cabin fever.

That's why outdoor activities flourish, such as skiing, ice hockey, curling, and especially ice fishing. To most people below the forty-eighth parallel, ice fishing is like hitting your head against the wall, in that it's not doing it in the first place that feels good. While I agree it's not for everyone, it must be experienced to be truly appreciated. Here are some basics to get you started.

First, find a spot on the lake where the ice is thick enough to drive your car without dropping through. If you're unsure, watch someone else go out first. Next, auger a fishing hole in the ice. An ice auger is like a post hole digger, a large, screw-shaped, spiraling, cutting surface you rotate either by hand or with a gas-powered motor. In the fun department, the power ice auger sits just behind the chain saw and way ahead of the power leaf blower.

You'll need an ice fishing pole with a reel, a monofilament line, and a bobber. An ice fishing pole looks like any angling pole, only it's much shorter because casting isn't an option unless you want to back up and aim for the hole. You'll need a skimmer (a heavy slotted ladle for clearing out the ice that will form on the hole) and a five-gallon plastic bucket to haul your gear and your catch, or "tonnage." For bait, use a minnow or leech on a hook with a brightly colored weight. The best fishing is usually just off the bottom of the lake, and a slight tug on the line every few seconds— "jigging"—draws attention to the bait.

Other ways to increase your luck include following feeding time charts or using depth finders and topographic maps of the lake, so you can set up over ridges and shoals.

Every fisherperson has a secret weapon. Maybe it's a lure that will make that fish react against its better judgment, whether by seduction, rage, or appetite, and will draw in that fish like a Lutheran to Jell-O. Some folks spray their lures with fish oil to take off the human scent. (Word of caution; keep the fish oil away from your beer, or you'll be tasting fish for a week.) Others have lucky hats or do a dance that doubles as a way to keep warm.

Keeping warm can be an issue where skin is often referred to as "exposed flesh." To stave off the cold, the best advice is to dress in many layers. Avoid wearing cotton because the fibers don't wick the moisture away from you, and if you sweat it will turn to ice. Wool breathes well, as do many new synthetic fabrics. Wear a hat and scarf: sixty percent of your heat goes right out your top. Get good boots. If you bought them anywhere but up north, you're probably in trouble. Battery-powered hand and feet warmers work for some people. I knew one guy who used red pepper in his boots because "if it works in your mouth, it'll work on your feet." There are many forms of ingestible "antifreeze." Some of the homemade varieties should be kept far from open flame. You do have to be careful because hypothermia is real. Remember the rule: if you are cold and upset, you're fine. But if you start feeling happy, and everything is right with the world, seek help immediately. That is hypothermia talking, and you don't have much time.

Most people opt for an ice fishing house, a ten-by-ten-foot house with a propane stove and floor holes in the corners for fishing. The holes are usually covered by plywood with hinges that can be flipped up. Some of these ice houses are luxurious, complete with stereos, TVs, kitchens, bunk beds, couches, even hot tubs and saunas.

Many fisherpeople use a "tip up," a gizmo that flips up a flag when a fish bites. This frees one to multitask: fish and play cards, fish and watch TV, fish and learn Spanish, etc. Other warning systems including buzzers, bells, whistles, car alarms, voice-activated computers ("I believe you have a fish, Dave"). I knew a band teacher who rigged cymbals to crash when a fish bit.

There is a great deal of pride associated with one's fish house. It is usually painted to reflect the owner's personality, whether it's love of a sports team or hobby or particular cause. Because of the environment, brilliant colors are an advantage, as an all-white ice house probably wouldn't be found until spring.

Lake Mille Lacs is the most popular lake for ice fishing in Minnesota. It's located in the middle of the state and is known for its abundance of walleye pike, arguably the best-tasting freshwater fish. Thousands of anglers move onto this lake every year. In fact, in one night it becomes the fourth-largest city in Minnesota. Besides the fishing houses, one can find bars, churches, a bowling alley. The roads are even plowed by local resorts that rent ice houses.

The fun of ice fishing is that you never know what you might catch: perch, trout, northern pike, muskie, crappie, the coveted walleye. Or you can drop a line down deep and try to snag something with a lantern on its head. Who knows what lurks in the depths?

I knew one guy who felt a tug, so he set the hook with a sharp pull on the line. There was a tremendous fight until finally the line pulled free and he thought he'd lost the fish. Up came a license plate. He threw the plate in the corner and re-baited his line. Suddenly he was hit with a moment of recognition. He ran outside to see the hole in the ice where his truck used to be.

There's something incredible about pulling a fish up through an eight-inch hole. You just don't know what you've got. It's like going to the fair, it's the lottery. What's going to come out of that hole? The mind wanders and one dreams as he reels. A whole world of possibilities opens up, even if you don't catch fish, when you sit on a frozen lake in contemplation.

Few sights are as breathtaking as the northern lights over a frozen lake. Or the serene stillness of a night at thirty below zero, or the sudden quake of the ice settling and cracking. During the day, the light from the outside looks like a cathedral. In the midst of isolation and beauty, it's impossible not to think great thoughts and drift into philosophies greater than ourselves.

My favorite story is about a group of twenty Russians in Siberia. These guys were out on the ice when the chunk they were fishing on broke free and headed out to sea. As the ice melted, their "lifeboat" became smaller and smaller. Rescue teams in helicopters were sent through foul weather to save the stranded men. But when the copters arrived, nobody would get in them. No way. The fish were biting.

• • •

WHICH BRINGS ME to Otto.

I'm standing on the road just south of Bemidji, in northern Minnesota, hitchhiking after a very productive ice fishing trip. I've learned that two things will greatly increase your chances of getting a ride when hitchhiking. You can make a sign that says where you're going, in this case Minneapolis. And if it's raining out or bitterly cold, you can take off your hat and coat and try to look really miserable. Someone will usually take pity and stop. The only trouble with this method is you really *will* be miserable. I take off my coat. It's probably thirty below zero.

The first vehicle to pass is a 1960s robin's-egg blue pickup truck. It pulls over to the shoulder just ahead of me and stops. The passenger door swings open. I run up to it and look in to see a guy who must be eighty if he's a day. He says his name is Otto. I hop in, throwing my pack and fish in the back. Otto tells me he's headed down to the Cities, but he's originally from Embarrass, Minnesota. He gets a serious look on his face and says, "It's French"—for what, he doesn't know.

I like Otto, and that's a lucky thing, because we're rolling down the highway at about thirty miles an hour, and at this pace it's going to take several hours to make this trip. I'm about to say, "Okay, Otto, this is good, you can let me off here," when he kicks it down and we're going about ninety. Now we're blowing past the cars that have been passing us, and I'm hanging on for dear life. I'm wondering how long a pickup of this vintage can go this fast, when Otto kicks it back down to thirty again. We crawl along for a while, when again Otto floors it. We're up to ninety in no time. Now, as we fly past the cars a second time, the drivers are looking up at me like they really want to know: "What are you doing?" I shrug my shoulders. "I don't know, he's driving." Sure enough, Otto backs it off to thirty again.

At this point, I'm wondering what the heck's going on. Otto says, "I bet you're wondering what the heck's going on."

I say, "Yeah."

He says, "Well, when you get to be my age, the first thing to go are your knees."

I'm thinking, "Otto, your knees are running a distant second here."

He says, "So one thing they can do is take those old kneecaps out, see they aren't any good any more. Then they replace them with these new plastic jobs." He says, "I had it done a couple a weeks ago, works pretty good." About that time he kicks it down and we're going ninety again. I see him pounding underneath the knee of the leg on the accelerator. Finally it pops forward and we're back to thirty again.

So we're going down the road, thirty or ninety, and Otto turns to me and says, "It's awful cold to be out hitchin'."

I says, "Yessir, I was up at Black Lake fishing."

"What did you get?"

"Well, for a while I hit a school of crappies."

"Those are nice eating."

"Yeah. But then I went deep and was snagging eelpout."

"Oh."

Now, eelpout have to be one of the ugliest fish on the planet. I know you shouldn't say this about God's creatures, but these fish are truly hideous. An eelpout is actually a freshwater cod, a burbot, that lives in the lower depths of northern lakes. The eelpout has no scales, just dark gray skin, a fat white belly, little beady eyes. Believe me, you wonder what's going on down there that would produce this fish. When one comes up through the hole, you don't know whether to cut the line or throw up.

Otto says, "Yeah, eelpout, they make good eatin'."

I say, "What, are you kidding, Otto? It's all I can do to take 'em off the hook."

"No," he says, "you just gotta know the proper way to prepare them."

Now, I've heard that eelpout has the nickname "poor man's lobster." I've just never known anyone that poor.

Otto says, "I'll tell you how to make it."

Otto's Recipe for Eelpout

Preheat your oven to 200 degrees.

Take one eelpout.

Find one oak board, at least two inches longer than the fish
    and wider on either side. Oak works best, but you could
    use a fruitwood like apple, too.

Drive a nail through the tail of the eelpout into the board.
    This secures the fish so you can

Peel off skin with a pair of pliers.

Take out guts, leave head on fish.

Salt and pepper to taste.

Place fish in oven still attached to board. Keep the tempera-
ture nice and low.

Cook for at least two hours. Let all the juices get to know
each other.

Take out fish, board and all.

Pull out nail.

Throw away fish.

And eat the board.

Bon appetit.

Thirty, ninety, thirty, ninety, all the way home.

Marathon

ONCE AGAIN THE END OF THE YEAR is approaching, and my unkept New Year's resolutions remain stacked up like all the firewood I would've cut had I kept the year before's New Year's resolution. At this point I've come to the conclusion the only way I'll get through them all is to believe in reincarnation. If I were honest, every year I'd just say, "Okay, this year I really have to eat more pizza, forget birthdays and anniversaries, and say at least five incredibly inappropriate things, no, make that six."

I keep making one resolution, though, that I am planning to do. I really want to run another marathon.

It has to be Grandma's Marathon up in Duluth, Minnesota. I do remember the last time I ran Grandma's it hurt a little, but the neighbors who saw me pull my car up after the race said my walk from the car to the front door was the longest hour and a half of their lives, a horrible sight, like a slow-motion accident they couldn't take their eyes off of. But the next time, I tell them, I'm going to try something different. I'm going to train.

I actually enjoy running. There's a "runner's high," a euphoria one gets from running long distances, that I hope to feel one day, and Grandma's is a great marathon. It's run along the banks of the mighty Gitche Gumee, Lake Superior, from the town of Two Harbors to Duluth. Some buddies of mine had run it every year and said I should give it a try. I ran cross country in high school and always wondered if I could finish a marathon. Six months after a New Year's resolution loudly proclaimed in front of witnesses, it was time to find out.

The gun goes off, and thousands of runners, a sea of colored shirts, bob up and down. It is a perfect day of forty-five degrees with a little drizzle, and in under twenty minutes I pass the starting line. Luckily, I'm packing plenty of Motrin in a plastic jar, I mean plenty. I sound like a mariachi band going down the road.

I first run with a cigarette salesman who entered on a bet with his buddies. He keeps wheezing, "It's worth a Winston," and filling me in on various surgical procedures. He assures me there's a couple of vertebrae in the human body they've found you don't even need. He tells me that monkeys are almost as smart as people. "There's even a monkey they taught to smoke, and there's this dolphin . . ."

I say, "Wait, they taught a dolphin to smoke?"

"No," he says, "what good is smoking gonna do a dolphin?

They taught it a language like radar. But a dolphin is not a fish, mind you, it's a mammal, like us." He starts to hack and has to stop.

But I feel good, talking to people, having fun, waving to the crowd, the cheering crowd, completely oblivious of the future. Halfway through they announce the winners. Somebody has already won? Oh well, I kinda knew I wasn't gonna win, and I still feel good.

All along the route, there are volunteers handing out water and juice to keep you going. But at mile fifteen I witness a sight I hope never to see again. I see this grubby hand sticking out from the sidelines with a huge glob of Vaseline dripping off it.

Now, a valuable friend to the runner is Vaseline. You need it anywhere you rub together, or are rubbed by clothing. If you don't use a heapin' helpin' of petroleum jelly, you can be guaranteed viscosity leading to thermal breakdown. So, lube up before the race.

I follow the glob down an arm to this little man with high-water pants, a three-day growth of silver beard on his face, and a huge grin, and he's saying in a deep gravelly voice, "Vaseline?"

The thought of taking part in that glob sends a shiver through me. Nobody is taking any. In fact, everybody makes a huge arc around the little guy, as if saying, "Eeee-wwwww, don't touch me."

I make it past the Vaseline man, but I can't shake him from my thoughts. One of the perils of running is the ability to dwell for miles on a subject, no matter how repulsive. And I picture the Vaseline man when they are handing out the jobs.

"Okay, who wants to hand out water? Who wants the oranges?"

And he's saying to himself, "Hang in there, don't jump, hang in there."

Until, "Who wants the Vaseline job?"

"Oh me, oh me, oh, oh, me!"

I finally come to a peace with the Vaseline man when I realize my legs have started cramping up, and my pace slows to a crawl. A tiny pear-shaped woman blows by me, reads the back of my shirt, and says, "Come on, Kling." Then, one by one, the entire assortment of the human race parades past. A guy dressed up like a clown, a naked man running backwards, a guy playing the xylophone.

Then this walker passes me, doing that braggadocio, better-than-thou hip movement thing. A walker!

I want to stop, but I'd resolved to *run* a marathon, not *quit* a marathon, so I forge ahead, looking straight down, one step at a time. Truth be told, if someone offered me a dollar to stop, I would say, "Deal." But they don't.

It's like one of those dreams where you want to run, but you can't. And I'm starting to cramp. I reach for the plastic bottle. All of the Motrin is gone and now I'm in pain and worse yet, I've got the Motrin monkey on my back.

And then, BOOM, I hit the wall. Now, whatever you've heard about the wall, believe it. It comes at about mile twenty-two, or for me, mile nineteen, and it is evil itself.

Pain can't describe it. You see your own death mask. You're laughing and crying at the same time. You will betray your friends. You will give the secret rocket-fuel formula. Anything. *When will the running stop?*

Then an amazing thing happens. All of a sudden, your mind takes over. Since your body is worthless, your mind says, "Get out of the way, I'm in charge now."

I've heard of people finishing marathons with broken legs, and I believe it.

George Bataille, the philosopher, said that after enough pain, one reverts to a sense of eroticism. It's true. Suddenly everyone in the world becomes inexplicably gorgeous. The world is as beautiful as the Jehovah's Witnesses say it will be. I'm dancing with the pandas. Some leather-clad biker guy yells, "Lookin' good." Well, don't I know it, I've never looked better. I give him my address and tell him I have a hot tub.

There are rock bands playing in downtown Duluth. People cheer and their cheers hold you up. I will guarantee the best-tasting orange you will ever eat is at mile twenty-two. The flavor explodes.

Then I look ahead and see the walking man. I can take him. I'm hurt, and I'm tired, but I have to beat the walker. "Beat the walker, beat the walker," becomes my mantra. With a half a mile to go, I take the walker!

Then I see the finish line. I did it, I did it. No, I'm still doing it. I'm doing it, I'm doing it, then I did it, I did it.

Two angels of the Lord approach me, each with a metallic-looking blanket under one arm. They hold me up, and I say, "What are you doing?"

One of the angels speaks in tongues, but the other one clearly states, "We've seen this look before." And magically, my legs quit working. Completely. I have no feeling. I know I don't look good anymore.

The cherubs of a merciful sponsor float me into a tent and give me a cookie and put me on a cot. There's a guy on a cot next to me. I ask him if he saw that Vaseline man. Even in his pain, he can dig down for one more shudder. "Eeeewwwww!"

Then I drive home, where the neighbors have made popcorn and pulled chairs up to their picture window so they can watch me walk to the front door. I hobble up the sidewalk, wondering if resolving never to make a New Year's resolution again counts as making a New Year's resolution. Inside I hear the phone ring, and I hope to God it's not the biker man. What was I thinking? I don't have a hot tub.

Family

MY GRANDFATHER ONCE TOLD ME, "Be good to your neighbors. There will be a day you will need them."

Dr. Martin Luther King Jr. once said, "All men are caught in an inescapable network of mutuality." And: "The good neighbor looks beyond the external accidents and discerns those inner qualities that make all men human and, therefore, brothers."

Even though I wasn't part of the struggle for civil rights in the sixties, I recognized it. I was born with what was called a disability. To me it was just who I was. Even though I could tell the world wasn't designed specifically for me, I felt like I was a part of it, of my community and my family. So it was always odd to me when I was treated like an "other."

Dr. King, like me, wasn't after acceptance. He was after recognition: seeing something of you that also exists in me. What is it that makes us belong to each other?

I SAW PART OF THE ANSWER in action when the Interstate 35W bridge collapsed a couple of years ago. In the midst of the television coverage, something catches my eye, something out of the ordinary. Is it in the sequence? What is it? A man helps children out of a bus. I realize what it is. It's not in the events, it's more the casting. The young man helping the children was Latino—Jeremy Hernandez. The children are African American, white, Asian American.

I knew this would surprise people watching the national news. Minnesotans' faces for years have seemed as white as our food. There have long been thriving communities of African Americans, Latinos, and more, but not in the northern suburbs where I lived as a kid or, until recently, in the small towns. My neighbor, a curmudgeonly old Norwegian guy, always said, "I ain't a racist. Didn't I live next door to a Finn for forty-seven years?" To some folks that's funny, but not to the old guy . . . or to the Finn.

News anchors reported that officials wanted to thank many of the accidental heroes, but they had gone home. Now this was typical Minnesotan. There is a work ethic here: you do your job and go home. Nobody would think of sticking around for a thank you. It's just what you do.

A pride came over me. I love that about my people.

I RIDE THE 21A BUS ROUTE that goes from Minneapolis to St. Paul through an economically challenged area of town. Stores along the street have new signs in Somali, Spanish, and Hmong, among the old ones in Swedish, Norwegian, and Finnish.

There's a woman on the 21A who always sits near the front in the section reserved for the disabled. She wears a button that says, "I feed my husband but I talk to my cat." Next to her is a bag of groceries. She talks to everyone at once about her friend Ruby. "She worked at the fair where you throw darts at balloons and this little kid comes up to play, well he was too little for darts, but Ruby gave him one anyway, and before she could turn around he'd thrown it, and it stuck right in her nose, well if you knew Ruby that isn't such an amazing shot, but she gave the kid his money back, which I would have never done, and I tell Ruby about lockjaw, and when did she have her last tetanus shot, it'd been over three years, and I told Ruby she better go in for that shot. 'Oh, I'll be all right,' says Ruby, but she was awfully quiet the rest of the night, and I caught her in the corner several times wiggling her jaw."

There's this kid who sits near the back of the bus, always talking to people only he can hear. The lady up front explains that he has an amazing brain. He can't tie his shoes, but he can name every city with a Kmart, in alphabetical order. She says if you're riding the whole route, you should ask him to do it, makes you want to travel.

One time a man gets on the bus and stands up front swaying, extremely intoxicated. He shouts, "Roger," and waves. Immediately, everyone on the bus knows two things. One, there is no Roger on this bus, and two, one of us will have to be Roger. Today, it's me. The man plants himself next to me.

"Roger, how you doing, pal? . . . Yes, you are too Roger,

Roger . . . yes, you are, yes, yes, yes." His eyes roll around like eggs on a ship. "Yes, yes." I can tell he's forgotten his argument but remembers he was in the affirmative.

"Lookit, two weeks ago, I had it made, beautiful job, full-time wife. Care for a smoke, woops, I'm out, you got one? How 'bout lending me some change, no sense getting uppity, sorry I'm alive."

Before he leans over and falls asleep, he's told me he was a CEO of a major company, a concert pianist, a place kicker for the Miami Dolphins, and if he told me his name, I would recognize it. Hard times can land on anyone.

Another time the 21A was at a stop. The bus driver says he'll be right back, then runs across the street to a convenience store. That morning I had been to the Social Security office, applying for disability benefits after a motorcycle accident paralyzed my right arm and left me unable to work. The first question on the questionnaire read, "What's wrong with you?" I couldn't bring myself to answer that one. Someday I know I'll need the money bad enough to answer it, but not that day.

We're waiting for the driver to return and get the bus moving when the kid behind me starts talking loudly, naming U.S. cities with a Kmart at a blistering pace.

A man up front, who had been holding his head in his hands, stands. Now we see this is one truly frightening man. It's his eyes. They have a blank, remorseless gaze. It is obvious that he is capable of anything. We're all thinking the same thing: "Please, just go out the door." But the scary man suddenly turns and faces the passengers. He points to the cat lady, smiles, says, "She's in charge now," dings the bell, moves toward the open door, and he's gone.

It's quiet on the bus. The cat lady is smiling, obviously pleased but not surprised she was put in charge. We all feel pretty good with the choice. There is peace. The driver returns and asks if anything happened while he was out. Nobody says a word, not even the lady, who still looks happy. We pull away, smiling in silent recognition, secretly knowing who is in charge, and you know what? There's nothing "wrong" with us.

WHEN I WAS IN AUSTRALIA IN 1987, a man explained family to me. He was a barrister, a lawyer for aboriginal land rights. He said it's hard to save the land for the indigenous people, because the government's rules for passing property to surviving relatives are based on heredity, and the indigenous Australians have a different family structure. In western culture, inheritance runs vertically like a tree, but for the people here, family trees run more like vines around the earth.

I said I didn't understand.

He told me one group has a unique familial system. When you are still in your mother's womb, you kick your first kick of life. She feels it and marks the spot on the earth where you kicked, then goes and gets the elders. Australia is lined with trails and paths, and you kicked on one of those paths. The elders determine what path that was, and you are related to everyone around the globe who kicked on that trail. He said, "Those are your uncles and aunts, brothers and cousins. Go to a village and stand in the southwest corner, which tells people you've come in peace. Sooner or later, someone will recognize you as a relative. Now, it might take them three weeks because you're white and not from here, but sooner or later, someone will know you as one of their own."

Recognition. That's what Dr. King was talking about. It's what makes us family. If we recognize each other as our own, suddenly there is someone nearby in times of need, there are more reasons to celebrate, feel pride and accomplishment.

When we set down the weight of fear, as Dr. King often said, we rise together.

In Love

IT'S SAID THAT THERE ARE two kinds of people: people who believe there are two kinds of people and people who don't.

It's said that there are two kinds of emotions: love and fear, and every other emotion is but a subset of those two emotions.

Aristophanes, the great poet of ancient Greece, asserted that the first humans had four arms, four legs, and two heads. But we had so much fun we began to defy the gods. Zeus, in his anger, split everyone in two, so now we each have two arms, two legs, and one head, and we are forever looking for our other halves. I like what Zeus said next: "And if you don't knock it off, you're going down to one leg."

We are creatures of love, for love, and to love. There is no higher pursuit than to accept and give love, to hold what is sacred in another and to protect another's solace.

And there is the euphoria of love. When we are in love, gravity stops being a law and becomes a suggestion. Our consonants desert us. A magic glow surrounds the world. We imagine our lives as perfect.

But love doesn't always work that way. I remember those cross-stitched wall hangings in my grandmother's kitchen, the "Recipe for Love: One cup kindness, two teaspoons tenderness," and all the rest. Like there was an actual recipe. But love isn't a formula, and that's why our lives are stories, not syllogisms—and especially love stories.

That's why when lovers look at the stars, they don't see a means to calculate a vector, they see the eyes of the ones they cherish.

THERE IS THAT BEAUTIFUL Bible verse from First Corinthians, the one that never fails to play on the emotions when it's used at weddings: "Love suffers long and is kind; love does not envy; love does not parade itself, is not puffed up; does not behave rudely, does not seek its own, is not provoked, thinks no evil; does not rejoice in iniquity, but rejoices in the truth; bears all things, believes all things, hopes all things, endures all things."

And it's true, love is all those things. But we're not. We're human, at times fallible, proud, scared. We want love because it holds all the things that we are often not. And when we allow love to rule our lives, we are given glimpses, moments of grace, a dance with the divine, the white-hot joy of being truly alive.

A psychologist told me that it's a sign of a healthy mind

when a person is curious and wants to master that which makes him curious. I feel love works the same way.

Love needs to grow and change.

It thrives in audacity and dies in carelessness.

I FIRST RECOGNIZED romantic love in Miss Jensen's fifth-grade class. The day before Valentine's Day, I carefully sort through my stack of Valentine cards. Thirty cards to a pack, thirty students to a class. Choices have to be made. What does this card say? What should this card say? And what should this card not be saying? Never give a girl a picture of a car, or a boy a ballerina. And when in doubt, go with a circus motif. A card bearing the words "Be My Valentine," is the most intimate, and therefore the most dangerous. You're stuck with four to a pack, so send them to one or two girls you trust and your best pals, with "You know what I mean" penciled in under the cartoon figure. Then, put the card in an envelope with a pastel colored candy heart, the worst candy ever invented, with phrases like "Why not," and "Uh-oh," and "What's that?" Phrases that seem to have nothing to do with love. Then you drop the envelope into a brightly colored shoebox, walk away, and never look back. Walk away. When I dig into my doily, tin foil, and red crepe paper shoebox, I find twenty-eight circus motifs and a couple of cars.

Later that day, we assemble in the gym for a social dance. All the girls are against one wall, the boys against the other. Miss Jensen blows her whistle, "TWEEEET." Then Miss Jensen puts a polka record on the metal record player, the record player you could hit with a medicine ball and it wouldn't skip. You could see vinyl peeling up from behind the needle. "TWEEET!" And we all come together to find partners and start dancing. I go looking for a partner, but none of the girls will dance with me. I am tiny. They are all so much taller, and their bodies are starting to change. They don't want some little head down there.

Many years later I was standing in the Outback of Australia. In the center of this vast, arid continent was a puddle of water. The puddle, on close examination, was teeming with activity. I asked the guide what was going on in there and he said these were thousands of tiny crustaceans, like shrimp, that lived in these dry areas. For about 364 days each year, they remain dormant in these hollows. Then one day it rains, and the puddles fill with water and the shrimp come to life. The puddles usually last only a day, so the shrimp have to do everything in their lives quickly: eat, sleep, procreate. The guide then explained this had been particularly wet year, and these puddles had been here for almost three weeks. I looked at the shrimp again, and they were definitely worse for the wear but still going at it full bore. Even if they wanted to, they couldn't stop the party.

I thought, that's junior high. There's junior high, right there in that puddle. In junior high, I started to notice girls, but they wanted nothing to do with me. For one thing, I was small. Not small . . . tiny. When I took driver's education, the instructor looked at me and said, "It's a good thing you live in the Twin Cities. You need both." And he shoved the Minneapolis *and* St. Paul phone books under me so I could see over the steering wheel.

I still couldn't pass the driving test. I flunked four times. Whenever I parallel parked, I ended up in the middle of the road. It looked like I worked for UPS. So I had to take a special driving course taught by the high school shop teacher.

THE MOST FEARED MAN in that high school was the shop teacher.

Ex-Marine, flattop haircut, lab coat with a pocket protector. He rode his bike to school every day. Spring, winter, fall, 30 below zero, here he comes, wind blistering his face, my brother and I standing in the cafeteria window watching him ride past while we sing the theme song of the Wicked Witch from *The Wizard of Oz*.

Every morning the shop teacher started out with a story to help "straighten us out." One day he said, "Boys, I was in the big one,"—Korea—"and once when I was walking down the road there was a hand, just a hand in the road, and there was a sandwich in that hand. Did I eat that sandwich? Damn right I ate that sandwich, best sandwich I ever ate."

Oh, man, I was paralyzed by fear.

And Scotch-taped above the lathe, the drill press, the table saw, every power tool in the shop, were newspaper clippings and magazine articles about children who were maimed on that particular tool. For my senior project I built a cribbage board that required using only a hand saw, a hand drill, and sandpaper. I didn't even have to plug anything in, but that didn't stop me from crying, "Oh God, I know I'll be the picture over the hand drill."

The shop teacher started the driver's education class by showing a movie called *Signal 30*. *Signal 30* was the code cops used when there was a fatality in an accident. Every scene ended with "Too late for this young man" and the jaws of life tearing open a car behind the narrator. One of four things happened to everyone in that class. You either passed out, threw up, never learned to drive, or loved it: "Oh yeah, that's me."

The shop teacher also taught the sex education class, and he showed a movie that was just like *Signal 30*, only it was designed for sex. And the same four things happened to everyone in the class.

In time, I finally passed my driving test, but in matters of love, I remained hopelessly confused. I know our pastor at church would say, "Look to Jesus."

I WOULD HAVE LIKED to learn from Jesus' example, but we don't know anything about those years.

The Bible is conspicuously blank on this period. Did he have acne? Did his hormones go crazy? Did he crash the family donkey? I visited a museum in Prague once that boasted they had Kafka's skull. Actually, they had two skulls, one from when he was a child and one from when he was an adult. I thought, that's how we think of Jesus: Child in manger and thirty-year-old Leader of disciples, no years in between.

In my teens, I really could have used some help. I wanted

to find love. I knew there was someone for me, but who? Who would like me? My body was definitely working against me. It was more than my height. My left arm is quite a bit shorter than my right, with only four fingers. I wear thick glasses—when the eye doctor says, "What letter can you see?" I know the big E is in the room somewhere, but I don't have a clue where. My friend Buffy used to say my knees look like I'm smuggling walnuts.

Oh, and my head.

I found out about my head at a Halloween party. We were playing a game called "Who can break the most pumpkins with their head?" Which pretty much covers the rules, as well. I kept breaking pumpkins, one after the other. Finally, a game I was good at. Then I met up with the pumpkin that was better at the game than I was. I hit it with my head and knocked myself out. When I woke up, my buddies said I should probably see a doctor. There is usually a good friend, almost always with glasses even thicker than mine, who knew a guy who knew a guy who hit his head, felt fine, went to bed, and never woke up. Somehow those stories have a resonance that exponentially increases as the next hours unfold. I told my mom what had happened and she drove me the well-worn path to the doctor's office.

Our doctor was Dr. Braun. He still had a thick German accent, which provided a strong sense of authority and calm when he gave his diagnosis.

He looked in my eyes and said, "Zey look fine, ja," then in my ears. "Goot."

Then he x-rayed my head from various angles and told me to wait in the room out front. I sat pretending to read a *Highlights* magazine, but I could clearly see Dr. Braun poring over the x-rays, going from one to the next and back again. Finally I couldn't take the waiting any longer. I walked back to his office and said, "Dr. Braun, is everything all right?" and he said, "You have ze head of an ape." I said "What?" and he explained to me that I had extra skeletal matter formed at the front of my skull, what was referred to as a "protruding browline," which in the x-rays did look like a thick mass of bone. He said I even had some skull "vere a little brain ought to be."

I asked, "Dr. Braun, don't you regularly see skulls like this?"

He said, "Not for sousands of years."

Doctors are always telling me how "interesting" I am, even when they've just met me. I've also learned when a doctor is happy it's not necessarily good news. Sometimes they're looking at a "new discovery."

As far as dating in high school, given the fact that, biologically, women are looking for a mate to pass down strong genes, I had to hope for a heck of a lot of "personality" to make up for lost ground.

THEN JUDY MARTINEZ moved to town. She was small like me, but beautiful. So beautiful. Judy Martinez, oh Lord, I would say her name over and over again. M-A-R-T-I-N-E-Z. I would trace her name on my notebook, replacing Big Daddy Roth Hot Rod drawings with her name. When she entered the room, I would gobble up every second, using seconds as fast as they could arrive, and holding them, trying to make the time stop just another second, just another second, Judy. The cracked cup of love, after all, is in constant need of filling.

And, when Judy tells me I look good, I believe her.

When a man in love looks in the mirror, he sees exactly what he's told. But when a woman looks in the mirror, she'll glance over and see who is doing the telling. When I tell Judy she's beautiful, she looks at me and says, "You think so?"

I say, "Yeah, I know it."

I was torn apart in love and rebuilt in her eyes, and like a star-crossed Italian lover, I would dauntlessly march into hell's gaping maw for her. She was like Sophia Loren throwing a basin of water screaming, "But Mama, I love him," until we ride off on a three-wheel Harley to join a circus.

But in love's game of Red Rover, Red Rover, tragedy is often called to come on over. Alas, Judy was transferred that spring to another school. Although we promised to write and stay in touch, our love grew pastel. Time and distance make for wonderful in-laws but poor lovers.

IN THIS LIFE A PERSON gets his allotment: a lot of circus motifs, a few hot rods, a couple of ballerinas, but precious few that say, "Be My Valentine." Luckily, I've been blessed with love anew, and I count the seconds with her as treasures.

I recently read an article in the paper about an elderly

couple in Chicago. The woman was crossing some train tracks, and her heel became lodged in the rail. Her husband rushed to her aid, yet despite their attempts, the shoe and the foot would not pull free. As a train approached, and it was apparent he would not be able to free her in time, the husband kissed his wife and said goodbye, and then held her as the train passed over them both. There were speculations as to the man's reason for holding on. Some said he could not bear to live without his wife. Some said he wanted to join her in eternity. But I feel he was thinking, "One more second, just one more second."

Coming Home

I'M IN AUSTRALIA IN 1987, performing at the Sydney Festival. Some of my favorite performers on earth are there, and what's more, they turn out to be great people. I am in heaven.

Another company visiting is the Druid Theatre from Galway, Ireland, performing a play called *Conversations on a Homecoming,* by Tom Murphy. It tells of a man who returns to his home in Ireland after making his fortune in America. It is a brutal, beautiful piece on the difficulty of a returning "hero." A huge hit at the festival, for good reason: Murphy is uncompromising and hilarious. The performers, as well, give it their all. Each character drinks five pints of Guinness stout during the play. They're using real Guinness. There are bathroom breaks written into the text, and you can tell these actors are running for it. Even at curtain call, there is a little tipsiness in the bowing. But they carry it off without a hitch. I'm saying here and now, kids, leave this method acting to the professionals. It's not as easy as it looks. My favorite is the stage manager, Padraic. After a performance, I notice he is a bit tipsy. He tells me he has five pints during the show, as well, to stay *in simpatico* with the actors. I say, "Padraic, you know, you could use root beer on stage. No one would know." He gets a profoundly serious look on his face and says, "Oh, you can't fake Guinness, man."

I went out with the Druids night after night. Luckily, they were five pints ahead, so I had a chance of keeping up. Our conversations ran the gamut. Tom Murphy in person was just like his play: hilarious and frustrating as hell. He would try to wind me up, night after night. I am very slow to anger—I don't just harbor it, I dry-dock it for years. But Murphy was unrelenting. Finally one night, he hit the tipping point. He decided it would be good for me to get in a fight. So he began looking for a likely candidate in the bar. After many failed attempts, he finally found him: himself. This was the last straw, and I went off. When I get that mad, it's like a blackout, and the next thing I know I'm looking at someone who is looking back in terror. Suddenly I'm looking at Murphy and he's grinning. In his mind, now he's ready to be friends. But I can't, I am still so mad at him. I know our détente is down the road a ways.

I have to say I felt a strong kinship to this company. So did the Australians. Our three countries share a great deal of history. We've all had similar relationships with England at one time or another. To start with, England couldn't send its ne'er-do-wells to America after our revolution, so

Australia became the next colony to get them, and somehow this included a number of Irish. It turns out many of us come from the same clay. My grandmother's maiden name was Catherine O'Brien. She made sure I knew we were of the Cork O'Briens and told the story of her father coming to America where he became one of the Indiana O'Briens. Somewhere back in my past are the Celts and the Druids, the keepers of the knowledge.

One night Steven Dietz, dear friend and the director of my play, came to me and said we'd been invited to perform at a hotel in downtown Sydney. It would occur on a Saturday after a performance, in the hotel's lobby; it would be great publicity and a way to get word out on the show. I said, "Sure, sounds fun."

That Saturday we approached the hotel to find people crowding to get in, lined up clear into the street. We couldn't even get near the door. Dietz says, "I'll find out what's going on." He works his way into the crowd and comes back fifteen minutes later carrying two Foster's Lagers. They're these beers that back in the States come in cans the size of oil barrels, huge beers. I ask if we are in the right place. He says yes, we are. Then he says he asked somebody waiting in line what the big crowd was about, and the guy said, "Last week the comedian Robin Williams did a surprise performance here. It was brilliant. And this week there's a guy who's supposed to be even funnier."

Dietz says, "Guess who that is?"

I say, "I hope you didn't think one of those Foster's was for you."

It was time for fight or flight. I take the two beers from Dietz and walk toward the hotel, finishing one before I hit the door.

IT SEEMS THAT THE ancient Celts had a similar view of the earth as some of the native people in America and Australia. It's sacred in the same way the body is sacred. More than simply home, it's part of them as they are part of it. This includes all the two-legged and four-legged creatures, as well as those that swim and fly through the air. It's also true of the trees and plants and even the rocks, rivers, and sky.

St. Patrick brought the Christian God to the Celts. In many ways the stories of each religion fit perfectly, so for some it was not a great leap. It also brought about one distinct advantage. In a land-based religion, one needs to be near the rock or river that houses the deity. But now, according to St. Patrick, God lived in your heart, therefore he was portable. Now the Irish could travel and bring God along, and travel they did.

But it's interesting that Irish people still speak so fondly of home. Not just "home," but of the land, the "auld sod," missing it so much that they don't ever feel complete when away from their clay. Even to generations removed, Ireland carries this sense of deep belonging. Grandmother O'Brien felt it, and I do as well.

What caused our ancestors to take flight? And what did they bring to the new country that we carry to this day? To answer this, I think of Zeus, our pony. He's a Dales pony, a breed born of the north of England, descended from native ponies of the isles. They're small in stature, which meant they could survive on the nutritionally poor grasses. They became all-purpose farm horses and also served in the dark underworld of the lead mines.

The more I know these animals, the more I am in awe of them. Opposable thumbs are highly overrated. Robert Bly once said he felt a certain neurosis developed in our nation when we stopped working with large animals. I believe it. You feel a calming force, a noticeable drop in blood pressure, when working with a horse.

Horses are prey animals, so everything they do is based on avoiding getting eaten. You cannot lie to them, because they read your body, not your words. All they know is you have eyes in the front of your head, like all predators; you are moving toward them; and you smell like meat. Talk about a relationship off to a rocky start.

We bought our pony as a newborn. The breeders mailed us pictures and wrote that his name was Zeus. When he was five months old, they brought him to us in a trailer from Canada to Minnesota. There he stood in the pasture. Tiny black colt, all legs and eyes, not quite sure of his surroundings. He seemed happy. Eating, playing. He loved the huge old Shire, Ben, who wanted nothing to do with him. So Zeus adopted Fritha, a beautiful Fjord horse, as his new mother. Fritha wouldn't necessarily be described as maternal, but she loved him immediately.

One thing was clear. Zeus had a great spirit. My partner, Mary, and I immediately fell in love with him, too.

We had him about a week when Zeus ate some white

snakeroot. For some reason, probably due to that summer's rainfall, the plant had an unusually high toxicity. Seven horses died from it just south of us in the town of Jordan. Little Zeus was down. Mary alertly ran him up to the equine hospital in Anoka. They ran tests and found the poison was eating his muscles. When it got to his heart, that would be the end. They gave him an IV to flush his system, but finally his legs could no longer support him. This is not good for a horse, whose organs are situated for standing.

The next day the vet called us to come in to see him. What he didn't say was he'd called us to say good-bye.

I sat in the stall with Zeus's head in my lap. This was the first horse I'd ever known, and he was leaving. Mary said, "Zeus, if you have to go, it's okay. But I wish you would stay."

She then said she needed some time alone, and left for a bit.

I sat with Zeus.

And wondered if this was it. "What do you think, Zeus?"

And he stood up.

The vet screamed, "Keep him standing. Keep him standing, every minute standing increases his chances of survival." Mary and I fed him apples, danced, sang, "The sun will come out tomorrow," anything for distraction. He stood for two hours.

The vet couldn't believe it. "If he gets back up, keep him up."

The next two days, he stood for longer periods.

The vet told us he had never seen a horse come back from that far. He said he thought it was due to Zeus's old blood, that immune system from ancient times. He said a modern horse would never have made it.

I wondered what genes we carry from our ancients, mechanisms for saving our lives, hidden immunities, inner fight, the knowledge of when to take flight.

There are clearly survivors in this world. I saw them time and again on the trauma floor at the hospital, as I recovered from a motorcycle accident in 2001. I never knew who would be a survivor. A tiny frail girl hit by a car on prom night amazed the doctors by fighting back to life, time and again; a tough guy from the streets, screaming in the night for his mother; and those who step from this world quietly, without a struggle. We don't know which one we are until we need it.

When he's stronger, we bring Zeus back to the pasture, now cleared of snake root. He's so excited, he runs toward Ben. "Hey, Ben, it's me." Ben is not amused. As Zeus runs to Fritha, his legs suddenly give out, and he tumbles head over teakettle. He gets up fast, freezes, and looks at me. Then he runs to me, I'm sure remembering I am the "apple man."

I say, "You're all right, Zeus," and he whirls around and almost kicks my head off. I watch him head back to Ben. No way is this pony leaving this world. Fight and flight all in one.

This summer Zeus turned five.

I'VE FINISHED THE SECOND Foster's, and I'm on the tiny stage at the hotel. The hall is packed. I'd never held a microphone before, always used a clip-on, and I'm trying to figure out the mic. I stand uncomfortably in front of everyone and wonder what I'll do. For many this would be a nightmare, but something profoundly sick in me kind of enjoys these moments. I am terrified at the same time, though, and the audience is clearly getting restless. Maybe I'll do a character from a play.

I ask if I can sit. "We don't care." Clearly, they're turning on me. And I know an audience can smell fear. I'll be gutted shortly.

When I sit down, about half of the heads disappear from view. "No, stand up, can't see you." I stand and move forward but the mic cord is caught on something. I pull it, no luck. I'm so terrified, I give it one great heave. The cord, wrapped around a chair's leg, flips the chair high into the air, and it then lands perfectly on its four legs. The audience, believing I did this on purpose, bursts into applause.

The rest of the night is magic. I can do no wrong. I can see Dietz looking around at people and thinking, "Don't you know he has no idea what he's doing?"

The next week I am asked to run a workshop on standup comedy at the Sydney Town Hall. "Of course," I say. Dietz just stares at me.

God bless Grandma O'Brien, I'm going in.

Shriners

WHEN I WAS THREE YEARS OLD, my two-year-old brother hardly ever talked. His vocabulary consisted of one word: "Not." That was what he called me. My mother figures it's because every time I asked for something, she said, "Absolutely not." So I became "Not." We were never apart, and I knew at a glance what he wanted. All he had to do was turn to me and say, "Not."

My mom would ask, "Steven, are you hungry?"

He'd look at me and say, "Not."

I would say, "Yes, Mommy, he's hungry."

"What do you want to eat?"

"Not."

"He'd like a sandwich and a doughnut."

"Not."

"Two doughnuts."

He was finally forced into learning the English language

the year I went away from home to the Shriners Hospital for Crippled Children. My left arm is quite a bit shorter than my right. Curled up tight and tucked in my armpit were four tiny fingers, no thumb, little and pink like a nest of baby marsupials. Most new neurological procedures, alas, have come from war, and thanks to technological advances during the Korean War, there were surgeries in the early 1960s that could not only straighten my arm but also untangle the muscles and possibly give some use of my fingers. So when I was three years old, I got in the car with my mom and dad—my brother and sister had to stay at home, so I was clearly the chosen one—and they took me to Shriners Hospital.

Now, thinking of Shriners brings to mind either the Shrine Circus, with clowns in helicopter go-carts, or the little, round, jolly, fez-pated men who come to your town parade, trash your Quality Inns, make you want to lock up your daughters, and then disappear. In reality, they're businessmen, part of the Masonic tradition, who provide a wonderful service. At their hospitals, children can receive free care, regardless of need, and the latest in surgical technology and rehabilitation.

All I knew was it was just me and Mom and Dad in the car, driving from Kansas City to St. Louis. I'm wearing a brand new powder-blue suit and my sister and brother have to stay at home. We arrive at Shriners and find Dr. Tippy in the lobby. Good old Dr. Tippy. I had met him on many occasions. Once, in an examination room, he had turned to my mother and said, "Interesting." Anyone who found me "interesting" was A-OK by me.

We're standing around in the lobby of Shriners Hospital for Crippled Children, me, Mom, Dad, Dr. Tippy, just us four grown-ups gabbing away the day, when I look at my mom and she turns away. Until this moment, my mom had never turned away from me—I could roller-skate down the stairs with scissors and she wouldn't turn away. As I look to my dad, he turns away. Then I hear Dr. Tippy quietly saying, "It's all right, Kevin, it's all right, Kevin," and when you're a kid, and an adult is saying, "It's all right," you know it is not.

Now my mother is crying, and I know it has to do with me, but I don't know why. I feel fine—in fact, good. Weren't we just having a good time here? I say, "I'm all right, Mom," because I am. This makes her cry even more. My dad helps her to the front door. I move to follow, but Dr. Tippy takes me by the arm. I would normally let out a wail here, but Mom is going through enough, and it deflates any chance for making a scene. Dr. Tippy then leads me into room with benches and closets. It smells like our cedar chest at home, where Mom keeps our baby clothes. A nurse takes me out of my new suit and hangs it in a closet.

"When you leave, it will be right in here."

"Okay."

She then leads me into a room with a metal table. I'm in my underwear, but nobody seems to care, and I certainly don't.

The nurse picks me up and puts me on the cold metal table. There's a low humming in the room. Dr. Tippy enters with some other doctors. Dr. Tippy says "Kevin!" like he's surprised to see me, even though I just saw him in the lobby. "How are you today?"

"Good."

The other doctors don't speak to me. They're very interested in my arm. I'm used to this. People in grocery stores, kids at the Old Woman in the Shoe babysitter service, a lot of people comment about my arm, but they don't usually touch it without my permission like these doctors do. After they squeeze and poke and prod to their satisfaction, they smile and tell Dr. Tippy good luck and pat him on the back. I'm happy for Dr. Tippy, and he seems very pleased.

Then the nurse takes some x-rays. There is nothing to fear. Perfectly harmless, I already know. Just pictures you don't have to smile for.

I'm led into a room full of very, very, very clean-smelling clothing. Everything smells the same, the-walls-the-sheets-the-clothes-the-food-the-people.

Soon me. I will smell like Shriners. When people visit or a new kid arrives, the smells are what get me first. We all gather around for that hit of new-kid smell. Mmmmm.

"You can wear whatever you want."

I look at the clothes. All the pants and shirts are clean, so clean there is a hardness to them, and it's apparent that many other kids have worn them.

"I want to wear my new suit."

"That's for when you leave us."

"When is that?"

"Hurry up."

The nurse is nice but not weak. I decide to carry the front of bravery a little longer.

"Here, try this."

With her help I choose a brown flannel shirt and blue jeans. They feel good in the hospital. With all of the pastel tiling and metal equipment, the flannel and jeans seem out of place in a very comforting way.

The nurse leads me into a large room with beds full of children with missing pieces. That's when the wave of acknowledgment wrestles through me. My arm, Mom crying, "It's all right," the prodding and poking, the whole morning comes into focus as I observe the room of incomplete children. This is a drop-off center for children with missing pieces. Dr. Tippy calls them my new brothers. Then he shows me a baby bed and says it's my new bed while I stay with my new brothers. A baby bed, with iron bars and a rubber mattress pad. I have my own real bed at home with a Lone Ranger blanket, and now I'm back in a baby bed? My brothers stare at me from their baby beds with expressionless faces. My voice trembling, I explain to Dr. Tippy, urgently but coolly, that this is all very nice, but I have to go home because you see I can't sleep in a baby bed anymore, and besides my brother, my real brother, can't talk, and he'll starve to death, and he'll scream bloody murder at night, and he won't be able to sleep unless I sing, "It's nighty-night to brother."

I start crying.

Dr. Tippy says, "It's all right, Kevin. We're going to fix your arm."

"Fix my arm? But that's what makes me special!"

Before I can convince Dr. Tippy I have been doing just fine with my arm, one brother, and real bed, a nurse takes me into another room. As I cry, she tells me that everyone is scared at first, but after a while this will feel like home.

"Not my home."

"And on the weekends your parents will visit you."

No, that's backwards, your mother doesn't visit you, other people visit you while you're with your mother, that's how that works. I can see that logic will not work with these people, and as the futility of the situation sets in, my crying subsides. I decide as long as I'm wearing someone else's clothes, I can pretend to be somebody who belongs here. But as soon as I get a chance, I'm grabbing my suit and I'm getting out of here.

Then I remember. I also have to get my name back. When we arrived, a man asked me to give him my name. I said, "No, I want to keep my name." He lost further ground with me by thinking that was funny.

Mom thought it was funny, too—no, "cute"—and proceeded to hand over my full name: first, middle, last. The name Dad uses when something is broken, or there's bubble gum in his pipe and he's somehow figured out it was me. I knew at the time giving over my name was a mistake. When I escape, I'll try to get it back. If not, I'll just have to leave it here where it will probably be cleaned and end up on a rack like all of the clothing.

The nurse takes me back into the room of children with missing pieces and sets me on the baby bed. On the BED, in CLOTHES. If Dad sees this, there better be a "Good Explanation" that includes a very high fever. I look over at the kid next to me. He is in a full body cast, covered in plaster from his toes to his fingers to his neck. He looks like an albino turtle.

"Hi."

The turtle can't move his head, so his eyes strain to see me. When he does, he smiles with his eyes looking at me from their corners. The indirectness of the gaze and his smile give him the face of someone who has happily done something wrong, is guilty and loving it. I smile back. This face is the first thing I've liked about this place. The kid's name is Gary.

"I'm Sandy," I tell him. As long as my other name is locked away, I figure I can choose any name I want, and Sandy has always appealed to me. "Why are you in there?"

"My spine is crooked."

"Oh."

"When I get out I can walk."

"Oh."

"It's not that bad."

It looks bad, but I can tell he's not lying. I think it's not bad for him, but it would be for everybody else I know. It would be for my brother. I rolled him up in a carpet once. It was his idea. He said "Not," so I did it. Then he started screaming. All rolled up in that carpet with a screaming head, he looked like an insane Pez dispenser. He wanted to kill me. "Not," "*Not, not*," "NOT, NOT, NOT." ("Unroll me," "*Unroll me*," "I'M GOING TO KILL YOU.") I was confused and still weighing my options when my mother ran in. "What have you done to your brother?"

But Gary seems at peace all rolled up.

"You'll get a cast, too," he says. "Maybe not as big as mine, but everybody gets one sooner or later."

"Not me."

I can tell he knows something more about my future than I do and it worries me into the night. During nighttime at Shriners Hospital for Crippled Children, nobody cries in their baby beds, nobody talks, but I can tell we're all still awake. The breathing sounds are of awake people. I try to talk with Gary some more, but the night nurse says, "Shhhh," and it's quiet. What's so good about having all these brothers if you can't go to sleep talking about the day?

I don't sing "It's nighty-night to brother." It's a song my mom made up so we could get my brother to sleep. He was afraid of the berts. The berts were headlights from cars passing our house that shone through our window and moved along the wall as they passed. This terrified my brother, and he screamed, "The berts, the berts," until my mom ran in and we sang. It goes:

It's nighty-night to brother, to brother, to brother.
It's nighty-night to brother, 'cause we all love him so.

He giggled every time we sang the "we all love him so" part. Then he fell asleep and his hand opened and doughnut crumbs fell out. People used to think my brother was angry because he walked around with his hand in a fist all day. The truth was, he was holding doughnuts, usually one of the first he'd seen that day, "Just in case."

So I sing "I See the Moon" to myself.

I see the moon and the moon sees me.
The moon sees somebody I'd like to see.
God bless the moon and God bless me,
God bless the somebody I'd like to see.

There are no berts, no brother, and I can't see the moon either. I say the nighttime prayer to myself. I say it slowly, trying to find hidden meaning. Most of the time I can say the whole thing in under five seconds. "Now I lay me down to sleep. I pray the Lord my soul to keep. If I should die before I wake, I pray the Lord my soul to take." Nope. Nothing. And I fall asleep on the rubber mattress. Falling asleep is like the moon, it feels like home no matter where you are.

NO MAN WAKES knowing who he is. Thank God. Then, with a sigh or a gasp, the realization sets in.

All the toys in the playroom are broken, either by the kids who owned them in real life or the kids who have already gone through Shriners Hospital for Crippled Children. I notice right away some kids have one toy, some none at all, and that one very small pale child has every toy he wants. He isn't playing with them. They are piled at his feet like he's the Christmas tree. He looks around the room at the other children. His face is expressionless but perfect: black, shiny hair, pearl skin with blue veins, blue eyes—huge blue eyes—and red lips. He is the closest human I've ever seen to the Charmin toilet paper posters. My sister has the whole collection hanging in her bedroom. I walk over and ask if I can read a Little Golden Book, *The Little Engine That Could*.

A perfect, pure, high-pitched note says, "No."

"You're not reading it."

"It's mine."

The unmistakable logic of power.

"I'll give it back when I'm through."

"No."

"Please?"

"No."

It would be easy to walk away. I've already read the book a million times at my grandmother's house and colored on some of the pages. But this isn't about a book. With my eyes locked on his, I pick up *The Little Engine That Could*. The perfect kid doesn't move. I slowly pull the book to me and start to turn. The split second my gaze breaks, his two henchchildren heave me onto the floor, take the book, and in expressionless, workmanlike fashion begin punching and kicking me. I scream for help but the other children do not move. In fact, they look more intently at their toys or projects or the floor. The henchchildren pound away.

At the Bluebird Shopping Center, when Mom dropped me off at Old Woman in the Shoe, the head babysitter said my brother was too young and not allowed to stay. While my mother argued, I ran to a toy oven and pulled out a plastic turkey. A bigger kid took the toy turkey from my hand and pushed me down. Steven tore loose from my mother's hand and started pounding the kid with his tiny doughnut-filled fist. He had to be pulled away. After that my mother always insisted my brother stay with me at Old Woman in the Shoe.

But my brother isn't anywhere near Shriners Hospital for

Crippled Children. As the henchchildren continue to pound me, I replace my body with the kid who owns these clothes. And while he takes my beating, I'm in the front seat of the car, riding back home with my Mom and Dad. It's nighttime, and we're riding through the Missouri countryside. The lights in the windows of the farm houses look like eyes twinkling. Every once in a while, one winks at me. I lean against my father, and I can smell his smell through his white cotton shirt. Mom hums along with the radio. My brother and sister are at home waiting to surprise me with a party. I am the chosen one. The car moves toward home, and I hum along with my mother, "I go out walkin', After midnight."

"Enough," says the tiny perfect manchild, and the beating stops.

Later Gary tells me, "Beware The Little Prince."

I say, "He told me I'd better stay in line, that he can make the nurses give me extra shots."

"No, he can't do that, but he can make it worse in here. Just ignore him. He'll stop after you're not new anymore."

I don't plan on being here that long.

"And," he said, "don't sing, the next time they pound you."

"Was I singing?"

"Yes. They would've stopped sooner, but the singing made them mad."

It's the same when my brother hits me. Never sing or laugh when someone is beating you. For some reason it just makes matters worse.

"Why is he called The Little Prince?"

"That's what the nurses call him. They always say, 'Whatever you say, Your Highness,' and, 'Mustn't upset The Little Prince.'"

I know even though someone is called a Prince, he doesn't necessarily act that way. My friend Kent Neil Winchester, who lives kitty-corner from our house, has a dog named King, and it doesn't act like any King I've ever heard of.

The nurses are all excited, not for themselves, for us. The Shrine Circus is in town. We aren't allowed to go, but the parade will pass through the courtyard of the hospital. The nurses tell us how lucky we are. We scramble to the windows as we hear the bands down the street, the face of a crippled child pressed in every pane. The parade circles below in the courtyard. Doctors and nurses and some older kids are in the yard below, waving to the floats. Gary's bed is pulled up next to the window but he's flat on his back and can't see.

"What's happening?"

With my face pressed against the window, I can see head tops of band members and clowns and soldiers. They looked like toys below. I yell at them to "Look up here," but I we're too high up, and the windows won't open. I stop yelling because other kids look at me like I am stupid. Gary seems more excited than anyone and he can't even see.

"What else?"

I tell Gary everything I see, but a parade looks very different from the sixth floor of a hospital, so I do some inventing with details from parades I've seen in the Little Golden Books version of *Toby Tyler*.

There are elephants, I tell him, and a giant, and monkeys, and a bearded lady. Then I begin to invent my own story. I know that if I'm walking down the street and a man pulls over in a car, maybe a hairy man with bad teeth, and he smiles and says he's my Uncle Carl and to get in the car, I should scream and run away. But if "Uncle Carl" pulls over in a story, I can get in and go with him no matter where that is, and in fact the story is usually better when I *do* get in. Gary laughs at the part where the lion breaks loose and runs rampant through the crowd, ripping the hospital staff to shreds and knocking over a lantern that sets the hospital in flames. The intent was for drama, but a laugh is a laugh in a hospital, and you take them when you can.

A little later some clowns visit us and scare the younger kids, but I have learned not to fear clowns. We have cake, and the clowns leave, laughing and honking.

It's very calm then, after the clowns leave. We are all sitting quietly around a little picnic table in the playroom, silently awaiting orders. Even The Little Prince Charmin seems compassionate in this stillness. Then it dawns on all of us at once. We are unsupervised. The nurses have left with the clowns, and there is no one watching us. In the brand-new stillness that comes with knowing we can do whatever we want to, one of the kids picks up some leftover cake and throws it into the eye of another kid. The kid with cake in his eye has both arms in casts, but manages to get some cake on top of his foot. The kid who threw the cake has to sit and wait because his legs are up against the wall across the room. The foot flicks the cake and pieces hit everyone and the fight is on. Cake flying everywhere. Gary is screaming, "Hit me! Hit me!"

The Little Prince Charmin is screaming, "No! No! STOP IT! STOP IT!"

But we can't. Soon paper plates are whizzing through the air. Cake in the hair, down people's prosthetics. Nurses rush in.

"Stop it. Stop it!"

The action comes to a standstill, but I sense there is just enough time to throw one more paper plate. I let it fly, and we all watch as the plate gently floats across the room and scores a direct hit on right forearm of The Little Prince Charmin.

"Got ya. Got ya," I yell.

But the room is silent. Everyone stares as The Little Prince Charmin lets out a blood-curdling scream.

Gary whispers, "Now you've done it, Sandy."

The nurses fly into action, putting The Little Prince Charmin on a gurney and rushing him out of the room. Another nurse calls for a doctor to meet them in another room, stat.

The nurses tell us quietly to go to our beds while they clean up. And we do. And pray for The Little Prince.

That was the day I learned what hemophiliacs are and why you can't hit them, even with a paper plate, because they might bleed to death. I also knew that's why The Little Prince did what he pleased. Everyone was afraid of him, afraid of hurting him. At Shriners Hospital for Crippled Children, you learn fast that mobility and dexterity have little to do with a person's standing in the pecking order.

Usually it is the other way around. It certainly is in the

outside world. We all knew this, and used it constantly to our benefit. We all knew when to cry, when to attack, when to throw a tantrum, and how good it made others feel to make us feel better. We also knew there were those who feared us and thought we were weak. Beware them and bring them to the attention of the others. We could suss out an adult in a sentence or two. I did. Depending on how someone commented on my arm I knew what to expect.

"What did you do to your arm?" This suggests that I am to blame for my condition, an assumption that must be corrected as quickly as possible.

"Nothing. I was born this way." Now it's an act of God, and this evens the playing field. Then to get them in your debt, follow it with, "It's okay, I'm used to it." Now you've let them know not only that you're okay, but so was their question.

If someone says, "What happened to your arm?" jump straight to, "It's always been a little smaller," because they already feel a bit compassionate and there's no need rub it in.

Any words like "shriveled," "deformed," "crippled," "withered" always have a negative connotation. It also shows they think they know why I was born this way. Even though I don't know what "happened," I make these people pay a little, simply by feeding into their fears. Make it worse than they already think it is, have a hard time with a simple task, struggle with a button or a shoelace. That does the trick.

Other children ask me about my "little" arm. I like the word "little," which makes no moral assumptions, so I tell them the facts and they always seemed to handle it well.

If someone is too bold and reaches for my arm, I pull away and it hold it like it's very precious and delicate.

But if someone is afraid of me hurting it, I'll show how strong it is. I'll pinch their finger, but not very hard, and say, "See?"

"Oh yes," they'll say, "very strong."

And everything is fine.

Don't try any of this on a nurse, a doctor, or your parents. New nurses maybe, other kids' parents for sure, but never a doctor. They don't put up with it.

In a way, I feel at home. Not in the hospital but in this community. At Shriners Hospital for Crippled Children, I'm in a world where everyone knows what I know. We are sealed in together like a city of mayors, and I've just laid out the baddest hemophiliac in the valley.

WHEN THE LITTLE PRINCE CHARMIN returns, his entire right side is swollen and bruised. He gives me the skinny eyes, and I know I'm about to pay big. I wish Gary was The Little Prince. He's in a body cast and by all rights should have the most power. But Gary doesn't care about power. He's happy. I'll bet he was born happy. I'll bet The Little Prince Charmin was born unhappy. And now his look tells me the rest of my stay at Shriners Hospital for Crippled Children is going to be a nightmare.

But before The Little Prince Charmin can exact his revenge, I get sick. I wake up the next morning with spots on me. A kid runs up to me and tells me I have the measles.

"The measles?"

"It means you have to live in a glass cage for three weeks, so you don't give it to the other children."

"Measles."

"It's not bad. You get ice cream, your parents can visit more often. And you can have toys."

"Toys?"

"When the nurse comes for you, every toy you're holding goes with you, because it has the measles, too."

I go immediately to the toy room, which is where they find me, buried in toys.

"Now we all have the measles."

All the toys come with me to the glass cage. For the next three weeks, all the kids come to visit. Not me. Their toys. I hold them up to the glass and the children talk to them through the glass. They tell the doll or stuffed bear or truck how much they miss them and what the their day was like, and to be good and not afraid. Toys in the hospital are our confidants, our confessors. When we're angry, they take the blows, when sad, they hold the tears. I learn a lot about my fellow patients over the next three weeks. Not The Little Prince Charmin, he just stares at me, memorizing me for later.

On March 18, I spend my fourth birthday in the glass cage. Mom and Dad visit me. They give me cake and make some of the henchchildren and nurses sing "Happy Birthday." The Little Prince Charmin is there, and I can see his lips moving to the song. I know he's not singing for me, but you just can't help singing when it's "Happy Birthday." It's a memorable birthday, but not for the reasons you would want.

I don't mind the glass cage, but I miss Gary. When I get out he is gone. He left a letter that a nurse read to me.

Dear Sandy,

I get to go home today. Back to our farm. I'll write to you soon.

    Your Friend,

    Gary

P.S. I'll miss you.

"And here's his address on the bottom, so you can write to him."

I started hiccup-crying.

"I don't know how to write."

"You tell me what you want to say, and I'll write it."

"Dear Gary."

I pause for a long time.

"Um." Thinking. "I miss you."

More thinking. "Um."

"Is that all?"

"No. . . . Um. . . . A Tyrannosaurus rex is big."

"Is that it?"

"Really big. The biggest. That's all. Love, Sandy. . . . Oh. P.S., when I go home my name is Kevin."

I feel better.

DR. TIPPY TELLS ME NOW that my measles are over, I can have my operation. All I remember is going to sleep and waking up with my own cast. Gary was right. This also prevents The Little Prince Charmin from hurting me for a while. Not even he can get away with beating a man fresh out of surgery.

Hippity Hop becomes my new best friend. I nickname him Hippity Hop because he was born with one leg and his mode of transportation is more vertical than horizontal. He makes everybody laugh because he is such a funny, goofy guy. You couldn't talk to Hippity Hop without wanting to laugh one of those lying-on-your-back tickle-laughs. And when I laugh, he laughs, and it can go on for a long time.

One morning I approach him and say, "Hippity Hop, I'm breaking out tonight. Are you with me?"

Yeah, he's with me, and Craig overheard, and he's with us, too. Craig will be a bit of a problem because he is in a body cast, so we tell him when we make it to safety, we'll get jobs and send for him.

"Okay."

That night, ten o'clock, nobody could still be awake. I slip over the bars of my baby bed and over to Hippity Hop's bed. He slides down, carrying his leg for silence.

"I'll need it in the real world," he whispers.

We sneak out into hallways of Shriners Hospital for Crippled Children, following exit sign after exit sign.

Finally. The front door.

"There it is, Hippity Hop, the front door. We're home free."

We creep toward the door on our bellies when . . . white shoes, followed by white tights, with little black hairs sticking through them, followed by white dress, then . . .

"Nurse! It's a nurse! Run, Hippity Hop!"

And Hippity Hop tries to escape, but they nail him right away. I can see him in the arms of two nurses, hopping up and down wildly.

"Save yourself," he yells. "Save yourself!"

Now it's up to me, running through Shriners Hospital for Crippled Children, running as fast as I can. I know to keep low. I saw a nurse try to catch a kid with no legs one time. The kid could move like greased lightning by running with his hands and dragging his body, especially on a freshly waxed hospital floor. The nurse could not catch this kid because she couldn't run and bend over to snatch him at the same time. So I'm running low and they are having a terrible time reeling me in. Finally, there it is, the front door again, freedom, home, Mom, Dad, Steven, Laura . . .

BAM!

They net me. They throw a net over me. And I'm inside this net, poking my fingers out the top like a strange slow-motion go-go dancer, and as I struggle, I remember watching a movie that had sailors who ended up on an island of giants. When one of the giants threw a net over one of the little sailors, they did this same strange dance, and I'd think, why are they poking their fingers up doing this strange go-go dance? Now I know, that's what you do in a net. I'm doing the strange go-go dance as the nurses wrap the bottom of the net around my legs and take me back and put me in the baby bed. But now they tie the net over the top so I can't get out.

The next day my grandmother comes to visit and when

she sees her little one in that cage, boy, does she ever let Dr. Tippy have it. "Grandmother, the net has to stay for my own good." Grandmother cries as she leaves, and I retie my own strings. What she doesn't know is that the net is the only thing between me and The Little Prince Charmin's henchchildren.

Every time Grandmother visits she brings another tiny plastic figure for me to play with. Mickey Mouse, Minnie Mouse, Goofy, Pluto, she hands each through the bars. I dream of Disneyland, paradise. And Pluto is my favorite because he has this thin plastic tail that's really difficult for my four-year-old fingers not to break.

Dr. Tippy got wind of this, I think. One day he said, "Kevin, we're going to take the stitches out of your arm, and it's going to hurt."

"Well, I'll scream and I'll cry."

"No, because if you scream and cry you might move suddenly, and we could make a mistake. You wouldn't want that, would you? For us to make a mistake because you were screaming and crying?"

"No."

"Besides, if you don't scream and cry, I have it on good authority that Pluto will visit you after you get out of the hospital."

I hold out my arm.

"Do your worst, Tippy."

So, one at a time, Dr. Tippy takes out the stitches that run from where my thumb was supposed to be, to my elbow, and I don't scream, I don't cry, I don't make a peep.

And when he is done, and it is time to go home, they read me a letter from my mother.

> Mommy hopes you were a big big boy today when they took the cast off. If your arm looks good to the doctor, you'll get a pretty new brace and we'll be so proud of it. Laura and Steven will want one like it but we'll say No, just Kevin can have one. Then you can come home Sunday. Mommy can hardly wait—yesterday we washed your Lone Ranger blanket so your room is ready. Remember grandmother and grand-dad Dysart will be there to get you. I mailed your new suit to grandmother yesterday so she will bring it. Have you been singing your songs? Here is some pictures of helicopters.
> We love you,
> Mother, Daddy, Steven, Laura

And then there's a drawing of our wiener dog, Stella.

On Sunday Grandmother and Granddad come for me with the new suit. This suit is mine. I am the first child to wear it. We drive to my home and there are my mom and dad and sister and brother waiting for me. My brother is as big as I am. He says, "Hello, Kevin," in perfect English. I go into my room, climb on my real bed with my Lone Ranger blanket, and wait for Pluto.

The Bunny

AT SIX O'CLOCK on Sunday mornings, I woke up to the sound of Herb Alpert and the Tijuana Brass blaring on the living room stereo. My dad's idea of reveille was *Whipped Cream and Other Delights*. I'd look over at my brother lying on his twin bed, just like my twin bed, with his Lone Ranger blanket that used to be my Lone Ranger blanket, and his charred headboard. That charred headboard from the time I said, "No, Steven, beds don't burn. A bed is too com-plex. Paper burns and wood burns, because they're simple, but a bed has too many com-po-nents." To illustrate my point, we wadded up three Sunday newspapers, comics, ads and all, and shoved them under the bed. Whoosh. There went that theory. My dad dragging the burning mattress to the front yard where he could get the hose on it and all the neighbors could see. We really got it for that one. Oh, the price of scientific inquiry.

This Sunday morning as we get out of bed, it suddenly hits. It's Easter—the Easter Bunny!

We rush into the living room for the egg hunt. To the untrained eye the room looks exactly as it should: nothing touched, nothing different. But we know better. The Easter Bunny has been here. The Easter Bunny took great care in hiding his precious eggs where no mere mortal could find them. Over the next hour, in order to excavate our treasure, we will have to crawl into the Bunny's mind, think his thoughts.

We empty sugar bowls, check edges of molding by hand (never trust the fallible eye). The Easter Bunny is the master of camouflage. Eggs the color of walls, couch covers, even trim. Eggs so well matched to the frames of paintings that they were only discovered years later as other artwork was being hung. One year the Easter Bunny shelled a bowl of peanuts, replaced the nuts with jelly beans, then gently re-glued each peanut shell. Every year the Bunny used a different kind of egg, so if an egg from another year was discovered, it could be dated and recorded. The Bunny was clearly proud of his work.

One autumn, our stereo stopped working. I remember the repairman standing in the kitchen with an Easter egg, circa 1962: "Here's your trouble, lady."

If you didn't approach Easter morning with all your senses on high alert and a screwdriver, you would come up short.

We knew this wasn't the only way to get eggs. One year our grade school announced that the Saturday before Easter, there would be an egg hunt in a flat field behind the school. We arrived to find hundreds of kids, kids we didn't even know from other towns, lined up and ready to take our eggs. The event was very poorly planned. You could see all of the eggs from the starting line, lying neatly in little green nests. Clearly this would be a "survival of the fittest" experience. The whistle blew, and it was a bloodbath. Crying children, dressed like bunnies, dodging the hordes. Rival gangs systematically taking out every quadrant of booty. Skirmishes on the pitch. When the smoke cleared, there were contestants refusing to leave the field, hoping against hope there was one overlooked egg. Children wandered blankly, like *The Night of the Living Dead,* until concerned parents ran to collect them. That was the only year the school sponsored an egg hunt.

But this Easter morning we've come up big, as the Easter Bunny was very generous. I am so happy the Easter Bunny didn't have that stupid naughtiness clause that seemed to put a damper on Christmas. With our newfound eggs hidden under the beds where no one would think to look, my brother and I put on our identical suits and go into the bathroom, where my dad has his hands held head high, palms in, in the "scrubbed" surgical position. But his hands are not scrubbed. No, they are laden with Brylcreem. Saturday night is bath night and we'd gone to bed with wet hair. We awoke with some pretty wild 'dos, and Dad is going to tame our heads with the little dab that did it. So into the tops of our heads he flies, rubbing in the Brylcreem, I can feel it burning my scalp. Feels good. Then out comes the black, personal, plastic, pocket-size comb. "Owwwww." Dad was a farm boy, plowing little red furrows in the tops of our heads. Then away with the comb and on to the top button of my white shirt, his stubby, farm-boy finger jammed between my neck and the shirt button. As he struggles with the button, he effectively shuts off my air. The edges of the world grow dim. As I inhale, my lungs are flooded with Brylcreem fumes. And off I go, off into the ether, off into the place I'd try to get back to many times in the seventies. Upon reentry, Dad scoops me up, then my brother, runs us out to the car, sits us in the back seat next to my sister, Laura, climbs in front, looks at his watch, rolls down his window, and . . .

Honk, honk.

"Gol-dangit, Dora."

Honk.

"Gol-dangit."

Dad's in a hurry because our church is in town, we're running late, and it takes over forty-five minutes to get there in time for the service. My mother is in the kitchen, frantically putting on the potatoes, putting in the Easter ham, setting the timer (*honk, honk*), making sure the dinner will be piping hot and ready just as we pull in after Sunday School (*honk*). She quickly checks herself in the mirror, jiggles the handle on the toilet (*honk*), and emerges through the front door—I'd swear on a stack of children's storybook Bibles—the most absolutely beautiful mom in the world, the stained apron wrapped around her waist that shows to Dad she's worked right up to the last minute. She stands a moment, a statue, unties the apron string, and lets the apron drop, then deliberately moseys over to the car, climbs in front, shoots my dad a look, and . . . we're in third gear by the end of the driveway.

Now I don't know if we are barometers for tension in the morning or if it's just being in a confined space. Whatever the reason, my hand wads into a fist and starts pounding my brother in the ear. Boom, boom, boom!

My sister wraps her hands over her new Easter hat and starts screaming, "The boys are fighting. I can't do anything!"

I don't know what she had to do, but apparently she can't do it while we're fighting.

Dad yells, "Boys, knock it off."

That's warning number one. It means nothing.

Dad yells again, "Boys, I said knock that off."

That's warning number two. That actually means a lot, but by now we're too far into the battle.

Finally, "Boys, I said, *knock that off.*"

Warning number three. This means action. We stop. "Dad, look." I give Steven a quick peck on the cheek. "See? We're pals."

Too late.

By this point my Dad has taken out what we call "The Claw."

The Claw is a human-looking hand attached to my dad's arm. We named it after All Star Wrestler Baron Von Raschke's secret weapon. We were not allowed to watch two TV shows: *The Three Stooges,* because we might "get ideas," which was true, they were brilliant, and *All Star*

Wrestling, for the same reason. One night, under the care of an uninformed babysitter, we caught a glimpse of Baron Von Raschke. His Claw always came out at the end of the match, because when it did, it was all over for his opponent. His Claw, too, had a mind of its own. There were times the Baron would use his other hand to try to hold it back, but The Claw never listened. It would attach to the victim's forehead, and that was it. Match over.

My Dad's Claw, with the strength of ten and the speed of a viper, launches into the back seat, in search of human flesh. *Our* human flesh.

We bob and weave, trying frantically to evade The Claw. I know if The Claw touches my sister and she screams it will immediately retract. She must emit some kind of enzyme or something. Then the idea comes to me, "That Claw isn't going to stop until it gets human flesh. Now that's either my human flesh or my brother's." So I grab some of his human flesh and try jamming it into The Claw. He sees what I'm doing and tries the same thing on me. This is my Sunday morning: in a flash, The Claw has latched on to Steven's leg. He screams, "AHHHHHH," hoping The Claw will show some mercy, but it never does. It's a sad fact, The Claw cannot stop squeezing until two fingers touch together through the human flesh.

"AHHHHHH."

And if you aren't getting The Claw, you sit and watch politely.

Finally the two fingers touch, and The Claw retracts.

I look over at my brother. To my surprise, he's reclining,

calmly and peacefully, as if to say, "It's nine in the morning, and I've already survived The Claw. How bad can the rest of the day be?"

We pull into the church parking lot. Five minutes late. We run through the lot, Dad's leather wingtips making that wonderful popping sound of crunching little stones. We run past the metal handrail where last winter I told my brother, "Tongues don't stick. Do you see any glue on there?" Truth be told, I wasn't as sure about this one as I had been about the bed. "You won't stick, go ahead, try." He did, and it did.

We make it past the metal handrail, enter the church, and silently shuffle into the back pew. We are treated to an anthem, a touch strong on the alto section, then the announcements, car wash on Saturday to buy gear for the Teens Camping 4 Christ. Now it's time to sing a hymn.

"Holy, Holy, Holy . . ."

All voices together except one. God gave Dad one note, and that's the note he brought to church. It was hard to define Dad's note. When he sang it, neither flat or sharp, it seemed to fall in that mythic area between two real notes. The note was more like a release of sound, sound that had been held captive so long it had lost the ability to work well with others. It flew from his mouth and inside your head and batted around like a bee that couldn't get out.

"Amen."

Thank you, God. The congregation takes a seat, and Dr. Richardson rises to perform his sermon. As he approaches the podium, the entire congregation settles back. From the back of the church, it appears the entire room lowers by a good two to three inches. Everyone knows this is going to take a while, and it is going to be on his "one note." Dr. Richardson hasn't even made it past the "amusing anecdote" when Dad's baby-blue eyes roll up in his head and he is out cold. At home Dad always snores, but in church he has a silencer. As he sleeps, it actually appears as if he's paying attention. When he nods off, his arm slides down his leg and his sleeve rolls back and he inadvertently exposes his wristwatch. Now my brother and I can have our breath-holding competition.

We've been waiting all week for this moment. We'd just seen the movie *Houdini,* starring Tony Curtis. In this movie, Tony Curtis holds his breath for three minutes in a bathtub full of ice cubes to practice for an underwater river dive. Three minutes? We figure we can do three minutes easy. After all, we've been practicing our whole lives. Besides, we are fully clothed, in the comfort of a church. The sermon starts, Dad's eyes roll back, and we warm up our lungs. In with the good, out with the bad, in, out, in, out, a great tension permeates the moment, only one will walk away with the coveted Tony Curtis award. There's the watch, the second hand hits the twelve, inhale, inhale, make it slow, inhale, inhaling counts as time, there, my lungs are full. I lock my lips in an airtight seal. Then the gulp technique, forcing more air down by gulping it like grape soda. I look at my brother. He's gulping, too, full of air. I can see Dr. Richardson's lips moving, but I'm so full of air his words are muffled. I look at the watch . . . thirty seconds. No problem.

My brother is making faces, trying to get me to laugh. He has "happy eyes," a false look of intense pleasure induced by oxygen depletion. I watch him with a very serious look on my face, so he knows this will not affect me. I also know facial expressions are burning oxygen he will beg for later. One minute. Still no problem. This is when relaxation is vital. Any mental stress can increase the heart rate and cost heavily. The worst thing you can do is think about not breathing, but when you're not breathing, it seems like that's all you can think about. I pretend to be engrooood in the hymnal, I pretend Dr. Richardson is saying something very interesting, when one of my eyes starts to squeak near the inside corner. It itches as air escapes. At two minutes, I close that eye and release used air through my mouth until the pressure is down to where the squeaking stops. My brother looks at me, eyebrows raised, excited that I might be dropping out. I shake my head "no" and point to my eye. He nods. Then he takes out one of the tiny pencils next to the collection envelopes and starts to draw. Outwardly a good idea, but I know my brother and this is a sign of desperation. He hates to draw. The only thing worse would be if he took out a hymnal. He hates to sing. He hates music. He is in the school band by force and refuses to practice. He can whistle, but they say there can't be a whistler in band. They say instead he has all the qualities of a trombone player. He hates the trombone. But now he's drawing in church, not a sin, but he's not drawing a picture, more like circles going around faster and faster in the same place.

At two and a half minutes I hear his body try to force air through the lips. The lips hold. He makes a noise in his throat, a vacuum gulp, like the noise was trying to break in instead of out. He looks around until our eyes meet. "Yep," I nod, "I heard it." Another gulp. His face goes stern. He's going to try all to beat this need for oxygen. Mom looks over and gives him a worried look. Still no release. His head drops to one side. He rolls it around. Mom looks away. She doesn't even want to know. I watch my brother suffer under his own will. Unbelievable, the human mind. More gulps, faster, like a drum solo or a prairie chicken calling a mate, as his hand shakes involuntarily. Then the other hand flicks as if touched by an electric charge, then his feet shoot out under the pew. Now his body is cracking like a whip from the inside. Still he holds on. He looks to me, eyes watering, body taut in a final convulsion. Just this side of consciousness, he lets the air out very quietly through his mouth.

Good man. Always let the air out through your mouth, never through your nose. If you let it out through the nose, people invariably hear you and wonder, "Who's having a breath-holding competition?"

Now it's up to me. Ten more seconds. I'm going to do it, the Tony Curtis is mine. Two fifty-five, two fifty-six, two fifty-seven. . . . "I'd like to thank my dad, whose watch made this possible, my brother, my mother—I love you, Mom . . ." fifty-eight, "My sister," fifty-nine . . .

"Praise God, from whom all blessings flow."

The Doxology. The congregation rises.

"Praise him, all creatures here below."

My dad stands.

"Praise him above, ye heavenly host."

I stand.

"Praise Father, Son, and Holy . . ."

But I haven't breathed in three minutes. The church takes one big spin over my head and I'm blacking out, cold. I drop like a rock, my head hitting the pew on the way dawn. On the floor I feel the blood reenter my head. In my delirium I can hear people shouting.

"He's had a vision. He's seen Jesus."

Except for Dr. Richardson. "Not in my church. Nobody sees Jesus in my church."

My dad scoops me off the floor and rushes me into the men's room. He sets me down on the toilet, runs a paper towel under the faucet, and hold it to my head. The cool water feels good.

Dad checks my eyes and says, "Holding your breath again, huh?"

How did he always know? He was amazing.

One year we have Easter dinner at the Edelmans', friends from church. They have two daughters my sister's age and an old cocker spaniel and a boy whose age is in between me and my brother. Their house is so neat it feels like a Petri dish, and I am clearly the germ. I'm not alone. I look over at my brother, who is staring down and mouthing the words, "White carpet, why?"

Their kids have Easter baskets. Brilliant! We always filled the nearest thing we could find—bowl, box, pan, pillow case, boot. An Easter basket is a great invention to remember. I ask how long it took to find all those eggs.

"Oh," he says, "they all came in the basket." In fact, his name is *on* the basket, so he and his sisters would know which one was theirs. This blows our minds.

"Let me get this straight. The Easter Bunny left an intact basket with your name on it?"

"Yeah, it does that every year."

"And you didn't have to slit a couch cushion or pry up paneling? It was just there?"

Clearly, the Easter Bunny isn't above favoritism.

We are on best behavior for dinner, but it is still fun. My brother finds a high voice that excites the cocker spaniel, causing Mrs. Edelman to quickly pick up the dog and move her into the kitchen where there is linoleum.

Their daughters put on a Beatles record and scream so you can't hear it. I am proud of my sister when she stares at them. I feel honored that she saves her screaming for my brother and me.

On the way home I think about the Edelmans and their Easter Bunny. I like our Easter Bunny. There is something better tasting about an egg that took a bit of work to find, even if it tastes a little like couch cushion. To be honest, I prefer matching wits with the Bunny. It keeps me sharp and prepared for shifting sands in my relationship with my brother.

I am curious about their Tooth Fairy, however. Something tells me the going price for a molar is higher in the city. I decide I'll wait for one of my brother's teeth to loosen and arrange a sleepover.

Rhetoric

MY NEIGHBOR, THREE-YEAR-OLD Johnny Greiling, is running back and forth in front of my house. He stretches his arms out in front of himself, he has a towel wrapped around his neck, and he's yelling, "I'm Batman, the animated version!"

Johnny comes into the house and heads straight for the dining room table. It's our ritual. I get him some water and a sheet of paper and crayons, and he makes me a drawing. Then he tells me what it is, and it replaces yesterday's drawing on the refrigerator. This time Johnny picks up a crayon and, with a look of concentration, works it all the way around, until he's drawn a circle. He pauses. I have just watched Johnny Greiling draw his first circle. He grabs the paper and runs out the door toward home. The next day he comes back with the paper. He sets it on the table. It's very wrinkled, and I'm pretty sure he slept on it. I ask if he wants a new sheet. No, he wants this one. Then John takes another crayon, and he puts in the eyes, puts in the mouth. And now I realize why this is so important to him. Johnny has drawn his first face. This picture is someone he knows, or someone he doesn't know, but now it is someone he can tell what to do. And things are going to be different in the world of John Greiling.

STORIES WORK THAT WAY FOR ME. When I can tell a story about something, it doesn't control me anymore. When I tell about something, it's from my perspective, in my terms, so I don't fear those things in life that are larger than I am. That's what stories do—tackle the big questions: where we come from before life, where we go after life, what's funny, what's sacred. And then, even if the question isn't answered, by asking it, we know we're not alone.

Stories, most importantly, show us that we belong.

As A KID, I WAS BLESSED with the gift of fabrication, the ability to weave. My "fabric" was made from invisible threads of speech and my early yarns were colorful if a little crude.

My Grandma Kling, a pragmatist, would reproach me. "Kevin, are you telling stories?"

I could tell there was a negativity in her tone but I proudly proclaimed, "Yes," and awaited my reward.

What I usually got, depending on the severity and fall-out caused by the tale, was the soap in the mouth. As if that could clean the stories away. To the contrary, it seemed to only serve as a palate cleanser for the next course. Finally

I wore Grandma down. The soap was left undisturbed, she would just shake her head and, in time, laugh. The sound of my grandma laughing still might reign as the most beautiful thing I've ever heard.

I was blessed with a life spent with laughers and fabricators. My family, experts all. In fact, I had to stop having intermissions in my shows because I could hear people laughing harder in the lobby than during my performance. My brother was out there, expanding on my stories.

I HAVE ALWAYS LOVED WORDS, especially the spoken word, whether used properly or regionalized, twanged or altogether altered. The Minnesota accent revolves around the long "O" sound, derived from the combination of Scandinavian, Irish, German, and Native American influences. Every region has its idiosyncrasies. People talk about a southern accent, but the South has a different set of rules for every county. It's the same in the North. I love how they say "youins guys" when referring to a group in Pittsburgh. It's the cousin of the southern "y'all," or "all y'all." One time a buddy said, "Us youins guys can beat youins guys in ping-pong." An invisible line runs across the U.S. It's especially distinct through Indiana; I call it the "Hon Line" because below it the waitresses all call you "Hon." I'm a big fan of the double negative, found in regions throughout the country. I'm elated when treated to a triple. The driver of a Minneapolis city bus once exclaimed, "Yeah, there ain't a day goes by I don't say, *shoot, I never seen that before.*" He hit those Minnesota Os like a walleye after leeches. How do you beat that?

The son of my friend Steve Alter came home from first grade one day. Steve asks, "Aaron, what did you learn today?" Aaron says, "Ask with our words, not with our teeth." Again, words to the rescue.

I learned early in life that calling out the word "Mom" got swift and immediate action, and that sometimes just saying "Mom" could make me smile, even when she wasn't in the same room. I learned the elasticity of words like "no."

Later I found that I could tell by the words people chose to refer to my smaller left arm whether they blamed me, my parents, God, or themselves for my condition. And with that information I could get what I needed from them. Word choice tells a lot about a person.

In junior high I learned about the humor in words: the laughter elicited when a teacher would say *homo erectus, bastard file, hoar frost, penal colony, sperm whale,* or *tufted titmouse.* When my mouth got me in trouble, I was fortunate to have teachers who discouraged me with a wink. How wonderful was that? Outright encouragement has not near the effect of those winks, because what use is a story if it doesn't contain a bit of subversion? In college I found that last night was only as good as your ability to tell about it.

Even to this day, I try to choose my words carefully. I have a relatively weak command of the English language, so to get an idea across, each word must be a hero.

This is why I get upset when words I love are used roughly and carelessly. Like the phrase *theater of war.* This bothers me. War has a horror that seems lessened, made unreal, by associating it with the artifice of theater.

Two words I love, *fool* and *clown,* are used interchangeably, but they are two separate beings. Shakespeare has both fools and clowns in his plays, and they are very different in nature. Fools have a foot in two worlds, an ethereal as well as an earthly quality, while clowns are firmly planted in a world parallel to our own. King Lear's fool gives good counsel because he connects the absurdities of two worlds. The clowns in *A Midsummer Night's Dream* demonstrate great examples of what not to do by doing it, but they would make horrible advisors, because clowns can't understand another's world. In many native cultures, clowns are a vital part of society. Living on the fringes, "contraries," they provide laughter at times when needed. They also present absurdities of a situation by showing their version. However, if the clowns are making more sense than the leaders, you knew there is a problem.

My friend Al, an Anishinaabe medicine man and wise fool, says that we have to be careful in selecting our leaders. He argues effectively that many of our past leaders have been clowns. Not good. He advises, "Always go with the fool."

THE GREEKS BELIEVED in two forms of truth: logos and mythos. Logos deals with logic, syllogisms, and theorems, whereas mythos finds the truths that live inside of story, the truths within. It took me a long time to learn that a story doesn't have to be factual to be true. Art is often called "truth told through a lie." How truthful are the depictions in the paintings of the Impressionists? Does van Gogh's work reflect a representation of the sunflower field or instill the serenity of a summer day in southern France?

WHEN ARISTOTLE SPOKE of rhetoric, he cited three forms of persuasion. We persuade through logic, through morals, and through emotions. Logic presents the arguments through the facts, morals show them through our beliefs about what is right and wrong, and emotional persuasion affects our hearts.

When most people are asked why they vote for someone or believe something, they point to a logical answer, relying on facts. In truth, logic is the least likely to succeed in persuasion. My fishing friends always kiss the minnow before putting it on a hook. I asked if it's superstitious. "No," they say. "Common sense, I don't want to jinx it."

It turns out, emotions get us to act faster than anything else. Fear especially. Fear of the unknown, of death, of the other, of losing what you have.

Rhetoric is trying to get us to perform an action, and its success is only determined by whether not we perform the desired action. Rhetoric doesn't care how it wins, it just wants to win. The purpose and use of rhetoric is the responsibility of the speaker.

THE ANCIENTS ALSO BELIEVED "the spirit" was found in breath. We "inspire" and we "expire."

"I am the Word," announced the Holy Spirit. The breath. Story lives in breath, in spirit.

The prophets spoke the first messages from the beyond

in forms of story. Religions transformed in later years as the word was taken from the breath, from the spirit, at times manipulated to serve a person or cause.

Even as a kid I was fascinated by literature that arrived from the oral tradition: Beowulf, Gilgamesh, Roland, the Bible. In *The Arabian Nights,* Scheherazade saves her own life for a thousand nights through the power of her stories. Others have stretched the language: Shakespeare and Pushkin creating words as they go; writers who provoked society, like Cervantes, Swift, and Voltaire; those who wrote with a voice, like Twain, Dickens, and Flannery O'Connor. I felt I could hear their words jump from the page.

THE STORY OF THE ODYSSEY was told for many years before Homer wrote it down. When I've tried to read the Odyssey, it has seemed disjointed. The story begins somewhere in its middle, there are a series of digressions and geographic leaps, narrators change from third person to Odysseus's first-person account, there are scenes with gods, then humans, then demi-gods—the plot is literally all over the map.

But when I've *heard* it told, it's another story. One night, in Utah, a storyteller began at sunset, and by sunrise the next day, Odysseus was reaching the shores of his beloved Ithaca. It was beautiful and chilling and obvious that the narrative was created to be told. The brilliant way the story unfolds holds the listener rapt. This, like all great works honed by telling and retelling, is held together by invisible threads.

In Celtic tradition, the bards of the ancient kings were

as revered as the top generals. The kings knew that history would know of them through the words that were passed down. Make those words soar, weave your cloak of immortality of the finest invisible thread.

The shanachies, Celtic storytellers, were the keepers of history in a tradition that began in the days of the druids and continued on long after Christianity arrived. They traveled around rural areas, administering a sense of belonging to the isolated inhabitants of the Irish countryside. A shanachie was welcomed into a home with a meal, and then the family and neighbors would gather around the sod fire. If there was news it was shared: a war, a bit of gossip about the king, a joke, a fable, history, sometimes all at once. If the shanachie was asked the question, "Who is king now?" the response might well start with, "Once there was a man called Adam and a woman called Eve," because the answer required a lineage and an understanding of past, present, and future.

I'M IN AUSTRALIA, the Outback, in 2006, staying with some of the Adnyamathanha at a place called Iga Warta. Adnyamathanha means "people of the rocks." Their culture goes back thousands of years. I'm walking with Cliff Coulthard, and he is explaining how virtually every plant has a use as food or a medicine. Suddenly what had seemed like a barren desert is a land rich in life. Cliff points to the landscape and says, "This is our Bible, our encyclopedia, and our supermarket. The land holds a story and we are part of that story."

An emu, a huge flightless bird, runs past. Cliff smiles and says, "Fast food."

He then points to a small rock formation shaped like a resting eagle. He tells me the story of the eagle and his nephews, magpie and crow. By story's end, the reason for that formation is clear. Depending on how it's told, inside that story are many lessons. It not only tells how the land was formed, it also provides a map where one might find a cave for protection. The story also describes the relationship between nephews and uncles, as well as other family bonds. Depending on your needs, age, gender, or family, there are layers and layers to this tale, layers I will never understand.

Cliff points again. He says through this valley, the rainbow serpent traveled and ate something that made him sick. His people have avoided that area for thousands of years, because where the rainbow serpent vomited, you will become sick.

And now geologists have discovered uranium on that land, in exactly the areas where the serpent became sick. Uranium mines have sprung up, replacing sacred sites. Cliff is worried soon they will take Eagle Mountain. He says, "If that mountain goes, we will lose that story." With the story will go the knowledge it contains. It's like the loss of a plant or an animal. Gone is its medicine, its nutrition, its gift. Stories are life.

I know things change and we live in a different time now, but these folks sustained this environment for over *forty thousand years.*

• • •

I THINK ABOUT MINNESOTA. I love my home, but often I feel more like a renter than part of the Earth. We all know how we treat things we rent. A buddy of mine says, "Yeah, a rented car will drive over anything." I want to learn those stories of our land, from the Dakota and the Ojibwe. I want to hear stories from our ancestors, my friends, and our kids. The Dakota say we need to listen to the children because they are closer in time to the Creator and remember more.

This gives me hope for the future. It gives me hope for the Earth. Maybe, in time, we will give her a good story. Until then, listen to your fools and watch those clowns.

Train

THE FIRST TIME I WENT to Seattle was on a bet.

My buddy, Easy Bob, and I are at the Terminal Bar early in May having a couple of beers and indulging in a pickled repast.

All of a sudden, Easy Bob announces that he recently enjoyed a delicious seafood dinner at a restaurant in Minneapolis.

I say, "There's no way, Bob, we're three thousand miles from the nearest ocean."

Bob says emphatically, "It was good."

"Impossible."

"Seriously, probably the best seafood dinner I ever ate."

"Now that could be true, on account of you've never been out of the state."

"Neither have you."

"We're not talking about me. Besides, I have, too. I've

been to Missouri, and I had to go through Iowa to get there so that makes two, Missouri and Iowa, and I also know you've got to go to one of the coasts for a really good seafood dinner."

"Not anymore you don't," says Bob. "This restaurant, they fly it in fresh every day."

"Doesn't matter. Seafood doesn't travel well."

"What?"

"Seafood doesn't travel well, it's a known fact I read."

"But it's here the same day it was caught."

"You're missing the point, Bob. Time has nothing to do with it. It's the distance. *Distance.* The further you take a thing from its natural habitat, the more the subtleties dissipate."

"Like a Texan."

Bob laughs with another guy who has no business listening in.

With Bob, the more abstract the theory, the more laden with great and complex notions, the less likely it will find safe harbor on his shores. Time and time again, life's little revelations are dashed on his frontal reef of stubbornness and unwillingness to learn.

Bob, face devoid of expression—further proving my point—says, "My beer is empty. You about finished?"

If I choose to continue, I can close my eyes and hear perfectly good concepts hit his forehead, then plop onto on the floor, dead. It's a waste of time. I might as well be talking about the photosynthetic properties of chloroform.

"Chlorophyll."

"What?"

"It's chlorophyll, not chloroform."

"Was I talking out loud?"

"Yeah."

"Anyway, my point is, you won't admit it."

"Admit what?"

"That I might be more of an expert than you in a given field that we both know nothing about. Like this seafood dinner. You don't know anything about seafood. Heavens and earth, man, your idea of sushi is a thawed Mrs. Paul's. And you'll never admit I'm right and there's nothing you can do that will prove me otherwise."

So that night we find ourselves standing in a boxcar screaming out of the St. Paul freight yards at seventy-five miles an hour, on our way to Seattle, Washington, for a seafood dinner. Me, Easy Bob, and my big mouth. Easy Bob has lodged the door open with a two-by-four board, because if the door slides shut, we're automatically locked in. "If that happens," Bob says, "chances are, the car won't be opened for another three weeks, and I figure a lot of unpleasantness could happen by the time the authorities find our bodies."

I can just see it. "Well, Sarge, wherever they were going, it must've been in a hurry, they didn't pack warm clothes or nothing. And lookee here, apparently the little one was trying to hurt the bigger one, just before they gave out."

I would give anything, if I owned anything, to sit down, but I can't because the boxcar is bouncing furiously and if I relax, in any way, shape, or form, it is likely I'll bounce right out the open door. I'm tired and angry, not so much at Bob, but because a couple of years ago some pals of mine helped lay this track, and at the time we all shared a laugh at the lackluster job they were doing and how much they were being paid. Now I hate them, and the memory of their laughter mixes with the rhythms and screeches of the boxcar. My legs absorb the erratic jarring. I don't know how much longer I can remain standing. Easy Bob looks like a puppet whose operator has nodded off, leaving him to dance helplessly on a slapboard. I want to call him a name but I'm afraid if I try, the next thing I'll say is my lunch. There must be a way to make this stop, a logic to the situation, a key that will turn this predicament off. I conclude the boxcar is trying to shake something out of us, a secret, or an object, and once the boxcar, or the spirit of the boxcar, has this thing, or thought, it will leave us alone. I empty my pockets. Nope. Then my head. I begin making confessions to God, apologies to the animal kingdom, all the while my lips mouthing the words, "Oh please, oh please."

At this moment, the romance of the rails overtakes me. Not that things get better. I simply realize that at some point or another almost all romance goes through a time like this. Finally, the legs give out, and I curl up in the corner. This could ultimately mean unconsciously bouncing out of the boxcar and into the ever-mounting lore of stupid things people do after a couple of frosty ones at the Terminal Bar, but I don't care, I don't care, and I pray if that happens I don't wake up at the last moment.

Then, as terrified and pain-racked as I am, the sandman

takes over, and I'm in the Land of Nod, where at a safe distance I witness visions of a seafood dinner dancing furiously in the mosh pit of my slamming head.

LESS THAN A DAY out of St. Paul, our boxcar is uncoupled from the rest of the train. We sleep through it. When we awake, we find we are in a train yard in Breckenridge, Minnesota. Bob says, "Don't worry, another one will be along any minute." It's three days before another train comes through. It doesn't even stop, just slows down. Bob says, "We have to catch it."

Even I know this is stupid. More than one Jack London or Bret Harte story features a one-legged hobo, once goodhearted but now ruin't and bitter by the cards he's been dealt where wheels meet rail. But after three days sitting in the Breckenridge train yard, I can see him hopping along right next to us: "Get me outta here!"

Bob and I run beside that moving train for at least a mile, seeking out a good car and a chance to leap up and in. The height of the leap is especially tricky because the floor of the boxcar sits just above the shoulders. All of a sudden, Bob yells, "Look . . . cardboard!"

I said, "What?'

He says again, "Cardboard!"

A big sheet of cardboard, perhaps from a refrigerator box, is just up ahead in the ditch. Bob says, "We need that."

"What?'

He says, "You'll thank me later—cardboard on the rails is worth its weight in gold."

We each take an end of the cardboard. Now we're running at breakneck speed, packs on our backs, next to a moving train, trying to shove this giant piece of cardboard into a boxcar. It goes up and in and Bob right behind it, like he'd drafted off of it. It was an amazingly beautiful maneuver, a Fosbury floppish hurdle that even the Russian judges would've awarded a 10.

Now it's my turn. I throw my pack in the car. I can't believe how heavy it feels, every step the straps have been cutting into my shoulders. It's a relief to toss it to Bob.

Then I jump . . . poorly.

My upper half makes it into the car, my lower half dangles below, legs kicking, dancing on stones and rail and ties. One slip and I'm sliced in two. Bob grabs my shirt and pulls me in, where I immediately start crying and laughing at the same time. I am now allowed to feel the fear of what we just did. Blubbering spit and snot, trying to form sentences with only consonants, hiccupping, tears making estuaries in my filthy diesel-black cheeks. It's the only time on our whole trip I want to go home.

I'm scared.

Bob is laughing. He goes over to my pack, opens it, and pulls out three huge bricks. "When you were asleep in Breckenridge I put these in your pack." He's laughing as hard as I am crying. "You should've seen yourself trying to catch this train!" He's now laughing so hard he's stumbling, arms out like John Wayne in *Sands of Iwo Jima*.

"I felt so bad watching you run, I almost told you."

I wanted to kill Bob. But part of the reason I don't, no,

all of the reason, is—that was a good one. I wish I'd thought of it. I have to laugh. It's that or homicide.

We then screw these large eyebolts into the sides of the boxcar, one on either side of the door, and stretch out our hammocks so we can watch the world go by. This is how we will ride for thousands of miles, watching America out of a boxcar. The rhythm is what takes you; it eases out every care in the world.

Bob starts laughing again. "God, I'm glad that's over," he says, as the train picks up steam, heading for Fargo, North Dakota.

Train deux, Mayday, Mayday

By morning the train is gently switching through the freight yards of Fargo. I wake up, alive, feeling pain in every muscle of my body. We're moving at a leisurely thirty-five miles an hour. I take a deep breath. My kidneys, sensing the all-clear, crawl back down from my shoulder blades. I then experience the adage, "Once you pee out of a boxcar you're hooked on the rails for life." It's true.

Fargo is rolling past. A billboard in town declares, "Welcome to North Dakota, Mountain Removal Project Complete." Bob is leaning against the door, his silhouette framing the portal, stooped in the question mark of a seasoned 'bo. I stand in the doorway opposite him and squint into the horizon. It's going to be a beautiful hot summer day. I look over at my companion.

He turns to me and says, "Uh-oh."

I say, "What do you mean 'Uh-oh,' Bob?"

He says, "Uh-oh, we're on an outside track."

I notice we are on the far right track of a series of eight or nine tracks.

Bob says, "The way I figure it, outside tracks go north or east, so that means we're headed for Grand Forks."

"We don't want to go to Grand Forks, we want to go to Minot."

"I know."

I'm about to say, "Well, what are you going to do about it now, Bob?" when I see my backpack fly out the boxcar door. It hits the ground and explodes. I see all my things flying through the air, my underwear, my shirts, my martini olives . . . another brick.

Then Bob's pack is flying through the air. His pack hits the ground. His pack explodes. And I'm kind of looking to see what Bob brought along when I see Bob outside the door. He's flying through the air.

And I think, "Oh, man, if I see Bob hit the ground and the same thing happens to Bob as happened to my pack, I'll never jump."

I turn into the dark boxcar and by the time I turn back Bob is gone. I turn away again. "Oh God, oh God."

I close my eyes and leap.

A FRIEND AND I HAVE an ongoing argument on the definition of happiness. She contends that it is the absence of fear and pain, a steady feeling of safety and comfort, whereas I believe it is a fleeting moment of euphoria, a swift reward, a goal rarely achieved by reaching or merit. This essential difference between her and me has directed the very different courses of our lives. For example, while she is at home asleep, safe in her bed, I'm out in the colors flying through the air at thirty-five miles an hour, and I'm never going to land.

And then I feel my pants split.

Then my knee split.

Then my head hit.

Then my knee. And my head and my knee and my head and I start to roll and it reminds me of when I was little and used to take my brother to the Laundromat and put him in the dryer and drop in a quarter. After a while I'd begin to wonder when his quarter was going to run out, but now I wonder when my quarter is going to run out. I keep rolling over and over, and just as I'm getting used to it I stop. As I drag myself to a standing position, I run a quick inventory: my knee is bleeding and my head hurts something awful. Other than that, good. I notice Easy Bob, limping in the ditch, putting his stuff back into his pack. I start putting my stuff back into my pack, and that's when I look up as the train stops.

Train . . . three . . . Mayday, Mayday, Mayday

IN MONTANA WE RUN into trouble. Times three.

First, we meet up with two guys headed for the Rainbow Gathering, an event held each year at a different national park. Thousands of hippies and counterculture folk connect in a festival of peace and understanding. It's like a Dead concert without the Dead.

These two guys are about our age and explain they're from Chicago, headed for the festival in Idaho. We travel with them for a couple days, sharing our food because that's what you do. They seem okay. A bit lost in space and time. I've known a fair number of hippies—I think I even was one for a while. It's not an easy lifestyle to maintain. Even the most noble intentions have a way of turning in on themselves, and poverty and controversy are better in theory than in practice.

The twosome explain they had a late start and actually were just barely going to catch the tail end of the festival. They had been informed these Rainbow Gatherings were utopias, teeming with Good Samaritans who had places to live, mellow wine, and righteous herb. Upon arriving at the Gathering, according to the plan, they would make friends and start on a new life. A life that included free food and a place to live, maybe a yurt. I ask what they plan to do for money and one of the men says no problem, he has brought some poems to sell if things get tight.

The next morning we awake to find one of the men, not the one with the poems, is in a fit of rage. He stands outside the boxcar door with a large rock in his hand. The rock is so heavy he has to set it down every so often to swing his arms. He's not practiced in rageful gestures, and his movement doesn't time out with his words very well, so he looks more like he's trying to shake chewing gum off of his fingers. His rage simply doesn't match his colorful attire, but he is bigger than either Bob or me and in this condition could actually hurt someone. He announces that he is leaving and we are to give him the rest of our food and money. We tell them we don't have much of either. I try to explain that the money is earmarked for a seafood dinner, but this doesn't seem to win him over to our side. I learn seafood is "murder" and to a grouper, I am "Hitler."

Finally Bob decides it's enough.

Bob is like that brother you fight with your whole life, but when the world turns on you, there he is, and you know you are safe. Mostly because if he does to the world what he's already done to you, the world doesn't have a chance.

The guy picks up the big rock and comes at Bob. I wait on the far side of the boxcar. I figure since we can't see his buddy, he's looking to ambush us from behind. I have a piece of wood to bop him when he peeks in the back of the boxcar. In the meantime I try to glimpse over and see how Bob is doing with his battle. The two square off, and then Bob says, "Wait." I'm surprised—the guy *does* wait. Bob reaches into his mouth, pulls out his teeth, gently sets them on the boxcar floor, and says, "That was close."

I've played rugby with Bob for years. There's a shelf by the door of the clubhouse just for teeth. Now I recognize those choppers, passed them dozens of times. I didn't know they were Bob's.

Bob smiles, kind of like a clam. "Okay, let's do it."

Now the guy realizes two things. *Bob has done this kind of thing before,* and *Bob is probably better at this than I am.*

The guy drops the rock, slumps to the ground, and starts

crying. He explains his buddy had run off in the night with what was left of their money, the poems, and the dope.

Bob feels bad, but he points out that the guy didn't think through his reaction very well. The guy apologizes and says he barely knew the other guy, never knew him when he wasn't high. Only when the righteous weed was getting low did he start to worry about what kind of person he was traveling with. He's right—you really don't know somebody if they're high all the time, and what's worse, they're usually smoking for a very good reason.

The guy now says he wants to stay with us. Bob says that would be unwise and advises the guy to try and catch up to his pal. Bob says he thinks everything will turn out fine.

The guy says, "You think so?"

Bob is sure of it.

I have a few stories that could shake his trust in Bob, but I keep them to myself.

Bob says, "Now go."

The guy thanks Bob and starts over the hill.

I stay awake that night clutching that stick, Bob sleeping like a baby. There are few things worse than a hippie gone bad.

WE GET TO HAVRE, MONTANA, and we're immediately met by the yard bull. A yard bull is the cop hired by the town to make sure nothing happens in the freight yard. That means nothing. Conductors don't want you on the train and the yard bulls don't want you getting off. Whatever you were before you got on the train, you are now riffraff. Yard bulls hate problems of any kind and unauthorized people of any kind. Yard bulls can kill you and sometimes they do. This yard bull holds what looks like a wheelbarrow handle without the wheelbarrow. He says he's had it with all these hippies coming through for the Rainbow Gathering. A professional hobo is one thing, but these goofballs getting killed for being stupid makes a place look bad.

He says, "You two weren't thinking on staying here."

We say, "No, we weren't."

He says, "That's good."

We say, "We'll be going as soon as the train pulls out."

"No," he says, "you'll be going sooner than that."

We gather all of our gear and the cardboard and walk toward the next town, fifteen miles away. Our train passes us some minutes later. We enter the hobo jungle and wait for the next train. Something made of rubber is burning, for warmth. We meet a very old man, actual years somewhere between forty to eighty, smoking a pipe. This guy could kill the "guess your age" guy at the state fair. The quite-possibly-old man is very interested in us. Where you from, where you going, do you have a house, what's your shoe size, what are you doing for Memorial Day? It's uncomfortable.

When a train finally arrives Bob says, "We're taking it." I agree.

But the next train is all flatbeds, no boxcars.

"Ooohhhh," the Q.P.O. man says, "you're stuck here for the night." He giggles. Giggles in a pitch not heard since the junior high locker room.

Bob says, "No, we're taking it."

"This train goes over the mountains," says the man. "You can't go over the mountains on a flatbed. You'll . . . " and he takes his pipe and starts bouncing it on a box. He bounces it to the edge of the box and then . . . off. Then he giggles.

Bob says, "We can make it." I'm with Bob. I'm not staying in that jungle.

We find some tie-downs used for keeping freight secured.

We lie on the flatbed. Bob puts the cardboard under us. "Told you you'd thank me later."

"I really wasn't thinking about thanking you, Bob." We set up the ties, one over our chests, the other over our legs.

The old hobo tightens the strap over our chests, then slaps the side of the car like the rear end of a horse. "All set, but I tell you . . ." He takes his pipe out again and, in front of his strapped-in audience, bounces it on the flatbed . . . to the edge . . . and . . . giggle. The train pulls out of the yard. The man waves a final goodbye. I'm still certain of our decision. Just ahead are the Rocky Mountains. The train builds speed. "Here we go," says Bob.

I've never been so scared in my life, but the rhythm of the rails begins and in under ten minutes I am lulled to sleep.

THE TRAIN TUNNEL OUTSIDE of Seattle is famous. It goes straight through the middle of a mountain, and Bob warns me that it will test me: "You will learn to be patient."

I quickly say, "I know, I know."

We enter the tunnel and it gets dark, then smells of diesel.

I put a towel over my mouth, trying to suck oxygen through the towel. I sing "Ninety-Nine Bottles of Beer on the Wall." When I get to no bottles of beer on the wall, I reload. Twice through and down to forty-five bottles before I see daylight. I look at Bob and hope I don't look like that, but I bet I do. I throw that towel away. I'll throw everything else I'm wearing away later.

But we've made it. Guys from jungles outside of Seattle wave, welcoming us to the land of milk and honey.

We've made it.

We have our seafood dinner at Ivar's, and Bob agrees it's the best seafood ever. I think we could've eaten the box it came in and been in heaven.

Bob gets a job in a tuna factory in Alaska and hops a ferry out of Seattle. He says we'll meet up back in Minneapolis at the end of the summer. He says I know enough about the rails now, and he's right. Even though I'll miss him, I do feel confident.

Once I get past that tunnel I'll be fine.

I'm all geared up and ready to sing twice through and down to forty-five bottles of beer on the wall, towel over my mouth . . . but I hit twenty-three bottles the first time through, and it's daylight already. On the way out of Seattle, you go downhill.

I'M GOING THROUGH MONTANA. Havre is just ahead and I'm sweating running into that yard bull again. The train is moving at a crawl because the train in front of the train I'm on has derailed. I look at the wreckage, boxcars crushed like beer cans. These boxcars are made of heavy gauge steel, and it seems impossible you could get crushed in one. Then you see a derailment and the fragility of life comes at you full face. Bob warned me to take cars near the front or rear of the train if possible. The middle cars not only give a much bumpier ride, they also get crushed in a derailment. He was right.

Suddenly a head pops into the lower corner of the doorway. It says its name is Ed, and can he come aboard. Boxcar etiquette. I say, "Of course."

Ed says he was on that derailment, second one of his life, the first was back in 1957.

"I'm generally not a drinking man, but I got off that train and went to the nearest liquor store." He drinks from a pint bottle and offers me some.

Ed has two teeth in his head, one just above the other. They look like goners, but he won't have them pulled, because "I like my steak."

The whole time I travel with Ed he cooks. We eat like kings. Full breakfasts. Dinners. He has learned every dumpster in the state and knows when everything is thrown away. Doughnuts for breakfast. Salads for lunch. Soups and stews at night.

Ed has a small bag, about the size of one of my mother's purses, with everything he owns in it. A hatchet is strapped to the top "for self-defense." Ed gives me a look that says, "I like you, but don't try anything."

One day we're passing through a freight yard. Ed says, "Gonna be a recession."

I say, "What?'

He says, "Look at them cigarette butts. Last time they were smoked down that far we had a recession." Sure enough, three months later, I'm back in Minneapolis, boom, we have a recession. Hobo economics.

Another day we see an eagle flying overhead. Ed says, "There is an inner spirit and an outer spirit in us all, the spirit as the world sees us and the way we see ourselves. That's why people judge us on what we can't do, instead of what we can do. They see us in terms of our limitations. But our inner spirit knows different."

I think, "Dang, man, there's more to this guy than meets the eye," then I think, "Wait a minute, that's what he just said."

He says he has a brother in Minneapolis, and I should look him up if I have time. Tell him Ed is fine. He never gives me his brother's name.

I say, "Don't you want to live in a house, Ed? Sure seems like you could."

"Oh," he says, "I gave it a try once in the fifties, but I kept getting antsy."

Later, he confided, "I did fall in love, once. But it never worked. Never could. Somebody has to love you, they have to love you morally, spiritually, and physically. Best I ever did was two outta three. So I hopped the freights and been here ever since, where I know how I fit in my world."

BEFORE WE PART WAYS, Ed gives me a name of a man written on a scrap of paper. Along with the name come social security and union cards and other IDs. I say, "Won't this guy miss this stuff?"

"No," Ed says quietly, "no, he won't miss it."

Then I remember something Ed said earlier, when I'd asked if he ever worried about dying out here on the rails: "Nobody dies on the rails. Ever."

Ed was giving me another persona, a means to money or food stamps, a safety net. This was one of the most precious gifts I ever received. "Say hi to my brother for me." And the next morning he was gone.

I still think of Ed on bitter cold nights. He told me he winters in the Fargo freight yards. It's thirty below and he's in a box. Wouldn't have it any other way. He said he was rich. I imagine he was. But I bet whatever he had sat just below that hatchet.

When I got off the boxcar for the last time in the St. Paul freight yards I cried. Not because I was hungry or broke or filthy or tired, but because it was over. I knew it was over and I would never return to the rails. I'm not of that stuff.

I would find someone to love me, someone I could love—morally, spiritually, and physically—and try to figure out how I fit in this world.

Mom's Story

THE CELTIC SCHOLAR John O'Donohue says that because humans were originally formed out of clay, we naturally take on the characteristics of the earth that was used to create us. Its terrain determines our personalities. Are you from a craggy cliff or peaceful meadow?

O'Donohue also claims we have an inner as well as an outer landscape. Often they are close in nature, but at times the two terrains couldn't be more diverse. When someone thinks they know me, they are surprised when subjected to hidden drop-offs, gorges, deep pools, quicksand—to my shifting topography.

My mom is not one of these people. When I was growing up, she was way ahead of my inner and outer landscapes. I tried to use my disability as an advantage, to gain favor through "pathos and pity," but she never bought into it. I often wondered why my mom, of all people, couldn't see what others clearly saw. With others, I could get my brother in trouble in a heartbeat by saying, "Owwww," then holding my arm and simply looking at him with a wounded expression. Adults especially came down hard on him. But not my mom. "Nice try," she said.

Mom's treatment would pay off later in grade school. If I was shunned, it really didn't get to me. I knew I was essentially the same as everyone else. There were things the other kids could do that I couldn't do, the monkey bars for instance, as there were things I could do that they couldn't, a spectacularly disturbing lip-curl trick. But as far as these being criteria for a subjective rating of worthiness . . . no, it never flew. My dad traveled a lot for business, so much of the raising of my brother and sister and me fell upon Mom. This was a role her outer landscape was well suited to—she looked the perfect young, attractive housewife—but her inner landscape was not. Her interior was designed for a less cultivated crop.

Mom tried all the established artistic outlets for the seventies. Every time a craze hit, she was on it: decoupage, collage, fondue, Barbra Streisand. One day she found an advertisement in the *TV Guide* for an artist's colony you could join from home. The ad said in bold letters, "You Might Already Have Talent!" and then gave you the option of reproducing drawings of Tippy the Turtle, Pete the Pirate, or a split-level condominium. An instructor from the school would then evaluate your rendering and determine if you did, in fact, already have talent. He spotted Mom's, and soon the basement smelled of paint and linseed oil.

When my parents divorced, my mom had a sudden and drastic shift. She would need to make a living. Both her mother and father had worked. Grandmother was in banking, the only woman in her business school at the time, and Grandfather was a county treasurer. Drawing on her pragmatic Scots ancestry, Mom decided to become a court reporter. She enrolled in community college and started taking courses to learn the basic requirements. But one day she sat us down and said, "Boys,"—my sister was by now in college—"Boys, I don't know what this will mean, but I want to become an artist." I think she thought this proclamation would be met with, "No! An artist? Are you insane? We forbid it. Think of the children, your future, what will people say?" But in truth we didn't understand, or care, what it would mean; we wanted Mom to be happy. We knew if we had approached her with the news that we wanted to be artists, which I did years later, there was no doubt she would have been all for it. Both my brother and I said, "Okay," and went back to the TV.

Mom took courses in photography, sculpture, graphic design. Left unsupervised, my brother and I would explore our own artistic avenues, mine in theater and his in the form of taxidermy. When I went to the refrigerator for a snack, I found one half of it filled with feathers and eyes, claws, teeth, and hooves, and the other half with dyes and fiber concoctions. I knew there was food in there somewhere, but I really didn't want to reach in and find out. My kingdom for a potpie.

Mom began bringing her friends home, bohemian types,

hippies and flower children. Some smoked pot and tried to convince me that littering was bad. A few were radical idealists, passionate and angry and ready to bring down The Man, after another helping of pot roast. Mom flourished, happier than I had ever known her, even though finances were always a bit iffy. Somehow she kept earning a living working in dress shops, silkscreen stores, making rock-and-roll T-shirts. She taught a college class while she was still in college, sitting at the dining room table at night, reading each chapter just ahead of her students.

She got a job at Munsingwear Apparel in one of the only non-manufacturing areas open to women, design. She worked long hours. To save money, she brought home factory seconds for us to wear. This meant there was a flaw somewhere in the stitching or construction. Sometimes a shirt had differing sleeve lengths, or a long stitch across the side or front. We called these "Frankenstein shirts," because the sections were clearly meant for different bodies. Sometimes we would take a prototype, try out a new line, and tell her how it felt or looked. We received underwear designed by a woman in the department who had neither a husband nor a boyfriend. Mom asked, "What do you think?" I said, "Tell her there really needs to be a 'front' and a 'back' in men's underwear."

We found our own courses, lived under the same roof, met each morning at breakfast. I went away to college, graduating just ahead of my mom.

A year after college I was touring Europe. I had six hundred dollars, forged documents and passes from some friends, and all kinds of great ideas on how to live in

Europe on no sense a day. I was in Hamburg, Germany. One of Mom's bohemian friends told me if things got tough, I should just stop and have a cookie. It's good advice. I bought my cookie and was walking downtown along the shops when I saw, in a department store window, one of my mom's designs. Inside I found a whole line of her clothing. Shirts, dresses, designs I knew well. I'd seen drawings of them all over the kitchen table, and the dye was in the refrigerator.

The clothes looked beautiful. The key to Mom's success was her innovation. In the seventies women like my mom found themselves competing with men for the same jobs. Business attire for career women had been available for some time, but women who were pregnant were still showing up to board meetings in duckies and huge bows. Mom designed a line of business maternity wear, and it took off.

When I was in Scotland, I sought out the village from which Mom's family took its name. Intensely proud of her lineage, she reminds all of my nieces time and again that they are members of the DAR, Daughters of the American Revolution, and before that, of Scotland. We are of a line. A line that runs clear back to this soil. I see that now. I had an incredible connection to the land when visiting Scotland. It felt vertical, as if from above, and shot through me and into the earth. I had never before experienced such recognition of place. This was my clay.

Throughout the village I met people who have my grandfather's eyes. At first, this was disconcerting. He had a stare: crystal-blue eyes that could freeze your knees and make you tell the truth. They could also twinkle at the end of a joke, usually as the only clue the joke had ended. Our family is known for our inability to get a joke right. I went to the post office. There they were, grandfather's eyes. The pharmacy, grandfather's eyes. At first these eyes made me miss him, then they began to somehow bring him back to me. I found myself speaking openly and personally to people I had never met. They went right along with me. When I said that my people were from this town, one man promptly bought me a pint of ale and told me to go ahead and hit him in the stomach, "Hard as you like." A high honor, I was informed later. Then they brought forth a jug that had dust on the top. They poured a glass. A beautiful burn. I was told the recipe was as old as my ancestors and this particular batch was old enough to vote.

I needed to tell my mom. I found a red phone box and called home. I told Mom I was in Dysart, Scotland, and everywhere I looked, I saw Granddad's eyes. She was silent for a long time and then thought I heard her cry.

I didn't say anything, then, "You would love it here, Mom."

"I know I would."

That was it.

I bought a cookie, sat in the park, and thought about Mom. The Scots are frugal, kind of nuts. Look at the land, sparse, unpredictable . . . these truly are my people. This is also clearly the clay of my mother.

I thought of my mom's designs, a true reflection of her inner landscape, of her journey, the reclamation of her self, a beauty born of necessity.

Softball

WHEN I WAS A KID, I played baseball for a team called Weaver Lake. Our win-loss record was zero and two. Zero wins and two years. Other teams had uniforms with names like Giants and Yankees, but our shirts always said Weaver Lake, proclaiming allegiance to the nearest body of water as if they didn't want to bring down the credibility of a perfectly good mascot.

We weren't really to blame. Granted, you could see with one look we were a team of future accountants and thespians. But our coach was Mr. Haynes. Mr. Haynes had never coached or played baseball in his life, and he figured we needed leadership. So he bought a book called *How to Play Baseball* and taught from there. The dotted line in the diagram of the throwing man didn't show clearly which leg was forward, so he had us throwing and stepping from the same side. You can throw a ball ten feet that way with a pretty good tailwind. Even our pitchers did it. We got creamed every game.

Mr. Haynes's undoing came one afternoon when we were losing to the Cardinals.

Now, from my years of organized sports, I know coaches know only three types of first aid. If you're hurt, a coach will say "Tape it up," or "Run it off," or "Rub it hard." No matter what happens: tape it up, run it off, rub it hard. Mr. Haynes was a "Rub it hard" man. If you took a grounder off the shin, he'd yell, "Rub it hard, that's it, you're all right, rub it hard." If you didn't rub it hard, he called a time out and came out and rubbed it hard for you.

This particular afternoon our third baseman, Mark Paddock, misjudged a ground ball. It was sharply hit and took a bad bounce and . . . *whack* . . . right between the legs. Ooo, the *worst* place to rub hard. But Mark wasn't hurt. The ball rolled harmlessly away, leaving Mark unscathed. Mark had bought a cup, an athletic protective cup. We'd never seen a cup. The kid on the other team got a home run because nobody went for the ball and Mark was basking in glory and the rest of us cheered and fell down in convulsive laughter. Mr. Haynes was livid. I said in a trained voice, "'Tis some form of majestic protective codpiece," and the next day we all got majestic codpieces. Hit it to me . . . whack . . . hit it to me . . . whack. Mr. Haynes never again achieved full control of the team.

A FEW SUMMERS AGO my brother calls me up and says, "Can you play softball this summer?"

I say, "Yeah, I probably could."

He says, "Great, I got the old team together, our Little League team, I got all the guys."

I say, "Steve, no, we were terrible."

He says, "You have to play. I got Dick's Bar to sponsor us."

Dick's Bar and Grill. The Medicis of softball. At the Osseo High School reunion, you can tell someone you discovered a cure for cancer, and they say, "That's nice." But if you say, "And I play for Dick's Bar," they say, "What, you're kidding! Hey, what are you drinking? Want another one? This is my sister. Let me praise you, for you are a god."

"Yeah," I say to my brother, "yeah, I'm in."

Our first game is a Memorial Day tournament, with seven teams competing for the trophy. I look at our team: they look the same as when we were little, a bit grayer and heavier, but it's the team. One thespian and nine accountants. The other team hasn't shown up yet, so we take infield practice. My brother hits a ground ball. Pocket protectors and reading glasses go flying.

I say, "Maybe we should have rehearsed."

"Too late," says my brother. "Look."

The other team arrives, strapping young bucks in uniforms, uniforms stretched tight over muscle and sinew. Our guys look shaken, but from years of playing softball I know young guys can be beat. They have the passion but not the craft.

And there are other subtle clues to consider. Watch out for church teams. Lot of aggression comes out on softball night for church teams. Also beware any team with "dog" in the title. Teams with goofy names, Jerry's Atrics or Foul Balls, are usually just . . . goofy. Teams with initials followed by the words *Construction* or *Refrigeration* or *Tool & Die* . . . look out.

Our team, Dick's Bar, takes the field first. The game stays close. And then around the third inning, the sun sets. Now this is May in Minnesota, so it's cold. It's thirty degrees. Freezing. We're all in jackets and stocking hats. My brother is in his duck-hunting outfit. Camouflage, boots, Gore-Tex hat. The score remains tied in the last inning. We take our positions in the field.

Before I pitch, I look around to make sure everyone is in place. My brother is in the outfield, lying flat on his stomach. All camouflaged. Like he's duck hunting in a blind. All he needs is a bunch of other softballs around him for decoys. I don't know whether to laugh or cry.

I pitch, and the batter hits it to center field. My brother jumps up, mimes aiming a gun at the ball, yells, "Boom, boom," and catches it.

Our team is now excited. We could win this thing. It took thirty years for this day.

The bottom of the last inning was spectacular. This is how I remember it.

I'm up first. And before I know it, I am cursed by Fate.

Two early strikes threaten to end my night. The other team is yelling, "Swing, batter batter, swing!" and I have been.

"Wait," says I. "Time out. For the gods' sake, time."

Then, grabbing another weapon that suits my grip, I say, "Quickly, men. Bring me tape, lash me to the bat, and stuff my ears with Bazooka Joe, so I may not hear their taunts."

My crew does as I bid, and stepping forward, amid taunts falling harmless now, I am . . . rewarded by three straight balls and an easy sailing to first base.

Cheers from my Friends in Arms.

But wait. This new island is guarded by a half-man, half-god. I know him to have but one eye, for when he does bat, his comrades shout, "Good eye! Good eye!"

The giant asks my name.

"Nobody," I reply.

"Well, Nobody, this is the last land you shall see."

But I catch the eye of the batsman, and we employ the hit and run.

"Watch Nobody!" shouts the giant. "He's running! Get Nobody!"

Ha ha, they are confused.

My comrade is out, but I stand safe on the next island, occupied by one who plies me with sweet words. Seductive words.

"You should stay right here," says he. "You're safe. You should be on our team. Your other guys are pigs. But not you. Stay, don't go."

His words of honey tempt, yet when our next batter flies out to right field, I tag up and run to third with all my might.

Safe now, I shed hot tears for the one who had sacrificed to move me forward. All of a sudden, I feel old.

The third baseman, would-be suitor of Victory, taunts me.

"You old man in rags, body old and weak, you're obviously from the island of Thesbos." And he laughs, making sport of me. "Victory is ours. You'll never make it home."

How dare he court the one I love. Young suitor.

Now my brother steps to the plate, standing like an oak, truly the son of our father.

Third-base coach, old trusted sage, speaks in good counsel: "Two outs—run on anything."

As my brother with mighty force swings his bat, I run, the path well-worn by past armies, warriors greater than myself. I run toward home, Athena, daughter of Zeus, at my side, bidding me on, until a warrior, ruddy of complexion, blocks home plate. I, smashing into him, send man and orb flying.

As I lie outstretched, bat still lashed to my wrist, Zeus himself, disguised in mask and armor, Lord of this Flat World, proclaims me safe at home.

Oh, how the heady wine does flow! The sweet lute plays!

The young warriors stand stunned, their wives and children groaning in grief and tears. Rending garments. Tearing hair. Shrieking like birds of prey.

We convene at Dick's Bar. High-backed chairs. Mellow wine in golden cups. And when we have put aside desire for drink and food (extra cheese on mine), and bathed in burnished tubs, and warmed in soft fleece, I recount the victory again and again, 'til Athena closes my eyes with the welcome gift of sleep.

When young dawn with her rose-red fingers colors the sky, I awake in my bones, old again.

THE BAT NOW SITS in the corner of my office, tape on the handle. I await my brother's call.

Wonderlure

I CONSIDER *THE BEVERLY HILLBILLIES* to be one of the finest examples of the television art form. Seamless performances, strong in characters and plot, high in entertainment value, and chock-full of sound advice and words to the wise. Its hero, and a personal spiritual guide, was the soft-spoken patriarch Jed Clampett. Lord Clampett (for it was discovered in one episode that he was indeed the Earl of Clampett) once said almost in passing, "If you're too busy to go fishing, you're too busy." Those words struck me. Granted, that's easy for him to say, with $156 million in Mr. Drysdale's bank. But still, he has a point. I am ashamed to admit that the last few months I have been too busy to actually *go* fishing, but thank goodness that has not stopped me from flipping on the television and watching one or two of those fishing shows. I feel strongly that a bit of leisure time, although brief and channeled through another, is essential for resting my oft-overworked Muse. My friend Marie calls this "composting," but it's basically lying around with a bag of chips watching another guy fish on TV.

These fishing shows used to have celebrities like Bing Crosby battling some respectable palm-sized sunnies, but now they have these experts—taut, tawny, and tanned, with neatly trimmed beards, wearing new flannel shirts just out of the box. They don't seem the type that reads for pleasure, but with calculated ease, they can deduce, enrage, or confuse a multitude of sizeable trophy fish into life-threatening action, all the while using only the fishing products they personally endorse. And every year they come out with brand new and improved gadgets that use sonar or radar or NASA space shuttle technology. There's the high-test fishing line that's not only invisible to the fish, but can also pull your Winnebago out of the ditch.

One day, though, there was this new host on a show, and he's got a pencil-thin mustache, and he's wearing a loud suit and tie. Definitely not a guy you'd want frying up your Shore Lunch. But he claims his new "Wonderlure" will not only catch the fish, it will actually change your life. He asks you to give this Wonderlure a try and see if once you've caught some fish—and you *will* catch fish—you don't feel better about yourself. And, when you feel better about yourself, you carry yourself differently. You're confident, aggressive, and people will naturally sense that and treat you with respect. Then he pulls out the testimonials. He read a letter from a guy in Cleveland who wrote to say he used the lure, and after limiting out went home and gave his wife a hug. She said, "What have you done with my husband?" After a season of unbelievable luck, he put away the bottle and was spending quality time with his kids. His marriage was saved, thanks to the Wonderlure. Another gentleman, with the confidence provided by a nice stringer of fish, went out and made wise investments, and they showed a helicopter landing on the roof of a building, which I guess belonged to the lucky fisherman. Another guy met his future wife at the tackle shop when they both reached down for the exact same Wonderlure. Another guy lost a hundred and sixty pounds. Another guy used the lure to find his long-lost birth parents. Story after story.

Then the announcer came to a letter that was hard for him to read. He took a deep breath and relayed the story of this woman's husband, a man dying of a terminal illness. This man had led a good life, but knew his time had come. He had but one last wish: to land one more nice one. But the Fates had conspired to see him time and again come back empty or with just a couple of measly perch. In a last-ditch effort, he purchased a Wonderlure, and with his clock winding down, came home with not one, but the limit of nice ones, all keepers. His wife wrote to report he had left this world in peace and had actually lived three weeks longer than the "so-called experts" said he would. Now the announcer is crying, tears streaming down his face. I'm crying too. I yell into the other room to my girlfriend, "Mary, maybe we ought to get one of these lures, honey, you know, just in case?"

She says, "Get two." She's going to use hers to save the rain forest.

Mon Uncle

WHEN I WAS A BOY, my parents sometimes sought a night on the town, and they almost always went out on their wedding anniversary. One year, locating a babysitter was left to the final hour. I watched my father, dressed in a tuxedo, frantically leafing through an address book and dialing through the list. When my beautifully adorned mother descended the stairs, my father informed her he had asked his brother to watch over me. He quickly assured her that all other avenues were blocked, and it was either his brother or an evening at home.

My uncle arrived shortly.

My uncle was thought of as a loose cannon, a loner. My dad used to say he had a penny in his fuse box. At family gatherings, his job was to watch the parked cars or tend the barbecue. Something outside. These tasks suited him fine, and his pork ribs were incredible. In confidence, he

147

explained the secret. "There are three things I never wash, and one's my grill."

When my uncle arrived, my father told him, "Just put the boy to bed, that's all. Maybe tell him a story."

"No," my mother pleaded.

"All right," my father said. "Read him a story, he has plenty of books."

No sooner had the door latched behind them than my uncle turned to me and said, "Put on your shoes, we're going out."

Into the night we walked, hand in hand, to the forbidden area of town, where the buildings were boarded shut and weeds grew in the cracks of the sidewalks. We came to an abandoned movie theater.

"Before it was a movie theater," my uncle told me, "it was a vaudeville house, then a church, a pawn shop, and a bordello. They say it's haunted by a magician who was stiffed by the management. Now hurry up," he whispered. "We're late."

We went around back and entered an auditorium. The seats were already full of people, smoking, laughing, and talking. Odd people, like my uncle, people who belonged in a house of memories.

The lights dimmed. "Hang on," my uncle said. The lights came up on an empty stage. Silence. Then off the stage to the right there was a *clump*. The audience tittered.

Then, *clump, clump, clump . . . clump, clump.*

Clump, clump.

Clump, clump, scratch.

Clump, clump, scratch.

People were looking at one another. What is this? My uncle shrugged. I don't know. Eyes back to the stage.

Clump, clump, scratch. And then something appeared coming from behind the curtain. *Clump, clump, scratch.*

"A boat," someone shouted. "It's a boat."

It was the prow of a boat. The audience laughed. The boat kept coming forward until a man appeared, rowing with all of his might, rowing a wooden boat across the stage.

"Hooray," shouted the audience. "There's our man."

The man continued to row, already perspiring heavily and breathing hard with every pull of the oars. The audience cheered him on.

Clump, clump, scratch. Clump, clump, scratch.

Every once in a while, one of the oars slipped. This was met with a groan from the audience. But the man persisted. *Clump, clump, scratch. Clump, clump, scratch.*

The work was enormous, the progress minimal. In time the crowd began to get restless. Some people started talking among themselves. Some started smoking. My uncle strained his neck. Surely there must be more. What are we missing? But there was nothing. The man continued to row.

Clump, clump, scratch. Clump, clump, scratch.

Finally someone in the crowd yelled, "Get off the stage."

"That's enough," yelled another.

People whistled. A wad of paper flew at the boat.

"Stop it."

"Boooo, boooo."

"It's all right, uncle, I'm having fun."

He let the air out through his nose and looked back at the stage. By now the audience seemed to have forgotten they were at a performance. They laughed, chatted, drank from flasks. The man continued. *Clump, clump, scratch. Clump, clump, scratch.*

Suddenly, my uncle turned to me, "Beautiful," he said. Now there was a smile on his face. I looked at the stage. Nothing was different. The man continued to row. *Clump, clump, scratch. Clump, clump, scratch.*

Then suddenly, someone yelled, "Look," and the whole audience looked up at the stage.

"He's going to make it!"

Sure enough, the boat was approaching the other side of the stage. *Clump, clump, scratch.*

The man now was completely exhausted, pale, with sweat pouring from him. Every stroke looked to be his last. Someone yelled, "You can do it. We know you can. Come on."

But as the boat approached, it seemed all his strength was leaving. *Clump, clump, scratch.*

Now the audience was roaring. "Come on, come on, you have to make it."

Clump, clump, scratch.

Now the man was weeping from exhaustion.

"Help him. What kind of people are you?" shouted someone.

"Someone help the man."

"No, he has to do it alone."

People clawed to get to the stage. Others held them back.

The nose of the boat was now inches from the curtain.

Clump, clump, scratch.

And then the man stopped and set the oars in the locks. No one moved for a long time. Then the man took the oars, and with one more *clump, clump,* pulled the bow past the edge of the curtain.

The place exploded, people screaming, "Bravo! Bravo!" as the boat disappeared behind the left side of the curtain. My uncle turned to me, tears streaming down his cheeks. "Don't ever tell your mother I took you here."

We walked home hand in hand, and he put me in bed.

"Want to hear a story?"

"Yes," I said.

And we talked and talked until we heard my parents' car pull into the driveway.

Flight

THERE'S A GENETIC MARKER in most Americans that separates us from the rest of the world. It's the "long gene," an anomaly that is found in people who broke away from their society. Explorers and adventures. Leapers before lookers. The *whatever-happened-to*'s missing from high school reunions, whose last words were, "Watch this!" or "What's this do?"

I used to go flying with my dad in his little two-seater planes. He always had a small, single-engine aircraft. Sometimes, when I was away at college, he'd fly down to my school, about an hour from home. As he approached the campus, he pulled back the flaps, let out some prop, and buzzed the school with this dish-rattling noise. I'd hear it in my history or psych class and whisper to the kid next to me, "That's my dad." And after class I'd run to the tiny airport a mile from campus where he was waiting. Then we'd go for a spin.

One time Dad picks me up from school and we're flying along the Minnesota River, enjoying the changing leaves on a fall day. Suddenly, in a blink, we're in the middle of a cloud bank. I can't see a thing. I look over at Dad, and as usual, he's shelling peanuts, looking at a map, drinking hot coffee, wrestling with his glasses, and tapping one of his gauges on the instrument panel.

All of a sudden, he turns to me and says, "Do me a favor, Kev, look out and see if you can spot the ground."

I frantically look out my window, still unable to see anything.

Then I hear my dad say, "Kev, it might not be down."

DAD WAS NEVER HAPPIER than when in flight. It was where he was in his element.

When I was in college he'd send me letters . . . well, not really letters, newspaper clippings, with headlines like "Actor Starves to Death in New York," or "Two Percent of Actors Union Employed," or "Star of Hogan's Heroes Found Stabbed to Death in Driveway." There was never a return address or letter enclosed, just a handwritten, "Georgette, send to Kevin" at the top. Georgette was Dad's secretary. I wondered, didn't he think I'd figure out where these were coming from ? But that was Dad's way of saying, "I worry about you in the Arts."

For years I felt Dad never understood me, but now that I'm the age he was when he was sending those letters, I'm beginning to feel he did understand me. He knew what it took to be a risk taker, and it was his way of saying, "You sure you know what you're getting into?"

I did. I believe the way I feel on stage is the way he felt in the sky.

WHENEVER MY FATHER had something of great importance to tell me, he did it in the car. It was like he needed a head of steam before relating important information. The facts of life, in a '67 Mustang. Moving to the country, white Mercury Comet station wagon. Divorce from my mom, metallic blue Chevy on the way home from a fishing trip. And although most of these talks were planned, sometimes he would simply take his eyes off the road and look directly at me and say, "You know, Kev, the day you own a pair of wingtips is the day I stop worrying about ya," or, "Kev, don't get killed just 'cuz you know how."

One time, on the way back from a sales call, he turned to me and said, "Listen to me, now. If you ever get a chance to be an astronaut, grab it."

"Okay, Dad," I said, "I will."

Now, I knew where this came from. My dad grew up on a farm, milking cows, slopping hogs, driving a tractor, never going anywhere except over to the next row. But when he was sixteen he learned to fly from the Clarkson brothers, barnstormers and crop dusters, Crazy Clarksons they were sometimes called. When Dad turned seventeen, he lied about his age so he could join the Navy and fight in World War II. He wanted to fly, and the Navy was the last branch still accepting pilots.

Unfortunately, Dad put on his application that he could type sixty words per minute. The war had already ended in Europe, and the soldiers returning home in droves needed to be processed. So Dad spent the duration of the war be-hind the controls of a Smith Corona. "Kev," he said, driving an '82 Chevy, "never learn to do something you don't want to be saddled to for the rest of your life."

He surprised me the most one day when he turned to me and said, "Kev, I'm going to Europe."

What, Europe?!

He said, "I always wanted to go there, and I'm not get-ting any younger."

But, Dad—I mean, up till now my dad's travel was the Midwest and that was it. I knew he liked to travel, but I always felt it was for the sake of movement, not to actu-ally get somewhere. This is why being an astronaut made perfect sense. Space travel is the ultimate in traveling for traveling's sake, but *Europe*—that's a *destination*. I could tell he had his heart set on it, so I offered my tried-and-true advice. I said, "Okay, Dad, lookit, you're going to England, bring an umbrella. I know this sounds crazy, but once you get wet there, you never dry off. I don't know why. And don't eat the food, any of it, especially in Scotland. I ate something there once, and I'll never laugh at the dog for licking the garage floor again."

He said, "But I got to eat."

I said, "For goodness' sakes, Dad, people from Scotland go to England to eat. Oh, yeah, and be sure to learn the language, a phrase or two. I've traveled the world over on two phrases. If you learn these, you'll be fine. One is, 'I'll have another beer, please,' and the other is, 'Sorry about the carpet.' You can go anywhere with those."

"Well, Kev," he said, "I'm pretty sure they speak English in England."

"Ho, that's what you think."

As the trip approached, I became increasingly worried. I drove Dad to the airport in my 1967 Chevelle, and now I was the one dishing out advice from the driver's seat. "Have you got everything? Passport? Umbrella, did you remember an umbrella? You got money? Pounds, you gotta bring pounds, yeah, it is real money."

I was a wreck until he returned. But when I picked him up from the airport, my dad had this huge grin on his face. "Kev," he said, "I swear it's the best time I've had since Nixon was in office. Lookee here!" And he handed me a stack of photographs.

"You took pictures?" I've never even seen my dad use a camera.

I open the pack and I took out a huge stack of pictures. The first photo was a cow, long matted hair, brown, staring right at my dad. The second photo was a cow, looked like the same cow but a different angle. The third picture was a cow, the same cow, the fourth, fifth, sixth, finally I said, "Dad these are all pictures of a cow." He said, "Oh, that's not just any cow, Kev, that kind of cow is where all the cows in this country came from, that cow is the great-grandmother of all cows."

Now my dad is bursting with pride. I continue looking through the stack of cow pictures from my dad's trip to Europe, and I realize my dad *had* gone somewhere: he'd gone home. The last picture is of a woman mowing her lawn.

I say, "Dad, what's that doing in there?" He says, "Look at that lawnmower, Kev, isn't that the darnedest thing? I wanted to get more of it, but I ran out of film."

NOT LONG AFTER HIS TRIP to Europe, my Dad took his last flight. He was diagnosed with cancer, and after a short, hard-fought battle, one morning Dad gave a final breath, and gently stepped from this world to the next. My brother was standing next to me beside Dad's bed, and he asked if I wanted a ride home. When we walked to the parking lot, I saw we were taking his motorcycle. After being up all night in the hospital with Dad, I knew the fresh air rushing over me would feel good. My brother was about to start the motorcycle when he stopped. "Did you hear that?"

I said, "No, what?"

He walked a couple of steps into the field behind the parking lot. "It's in here." He shook a bush—and a pheasant rooster got up.

It flew high up and over a grove of trees, and then glided over a cornfield into the sunrise. We stood there on that cool spring morning, squinting into the sun, watching the pheasant fly. It was beautiful . . . and then it was gone.

Demo Derby

I LOVE VISITING MY MOM on the Fourth of July. Her small town has a parade that's over and done in five minutes, so everyone stays seated and the parade turns around and walks past again. Everyone then follows the parade to the park, where there is usually a long speech in the town square next to the cannon. Why there is a cannon in northern Wisconsin, I don't know, but if it makes people feel safer, then it's doing its job. The speaker talks about forefathers and -mothers and struggles and sacrifices and somehow, at some point, you are guaranteed to tear up. One year they read the Declaration of Independence, but everyone got so agitated they've gone back to a more nostalgic approach. There are picnics, sack races, horseshoes. The squirrels know it's just this one day, so they don't cause a ruckus. The best part is the evening fireworks. Every year the argument ensues: should they be fired off from this side of the lake, or the far side? Every year, this side of the lake wins, and even though they say they've moved back farther from last year, ashes and embers still rain on the crowd. People "in the know"—those who have attended before—bring umbrellas, newcomers take to using blankets they brought to sit on for protection. Sometimes an errant rocket will set part of the field on fire. The crowd takes a break from the "rockets' red glare" to watch the silhouette of an attendant reluctantly dump some of his beer on the blaze. Once it's extinguished, there is a cheer for the man, who raises his arms in triumph and finishes what the fire did not get. There are oohs and aaahs and a general agreement this display was better than last year's.

LAST FOURTH OF JULY, as a mother-and-son kind of deal, I took my mom to the Demolition Derby competition at the Ashland County Fair in Wisconsin. The poster in the Kwik-Stop promised thrills, spills, chills. The picture showed cars crashing into each other, like a multiple exposure photo of an evening at the liquor store parking lot.

We take our seats in the bleachers. The cars face each other in two rows. The rules are simple. Crash into each other until only one car moves, and that's the winner. Oh, but it is so much more. It's a medieval joust. It's the Roman Coliseum. It's oil and gas and steel. It's America.

The drivers, like knights of old, approach the arena covered in armor from head to toe. Their steeds have all the glass removed for safety reasons, and are decorated for the event. Half of them proclaim allegiance to places like

Dave's Taxidermy and Oedipus Wrecking Service. The other half, driven by women, are decorated in pinks and greens announcing Jennie's Hair Design, or A Sister's Love Coffee and Bookstore. One gentlemen gets in an all-black car with 3:16 on the top and words adorning the sides: "Say Your Prayers," "Powered by God," "Show No Mercy," and "Do Unto Others." Clearly, he has the blessing of the Lord.

The people next to us are a happy-go-lucky, round-faced family that do the derby to fill up the time that isn't deer hunting season. Their son, Ronnie, is in the competition. My mom says, "You let your son out there? Aren't you worried?"

They look at her blankly. "About Ronnie?" Mom obviously doesn't know Ronnie. The dad says, "You shoulda seen him before. This saved him, I swear. He was gonna hurt somebody."

Ronnie's mom is worried, though; she informs us his right rear strut is weak. She says, "Somebody hits him there, and I tell you, it's good night nurse."

The whistle blows and Ronnie's car screams across the field in reverse and takes out a guy's radiator, rendering him dead in a world of hissing steam.

"Atta boy, Ronnie," yells his family. "Whoohoo!"

All of a sudden, my mom says, "Oh, my God."

"What, Mom?" I say.

She says, "There's my old Nova."

"What?"

"That Nova from Jennie's Hair Design, that's my old car, I swear."

"No way."

"Yes. Oh, no," she says. "What a nightmare. Do you know the care I gave that car? I can't look."

"Mom, there's lots of Novas like that."

"I ought to know my own car. Look out!" she yells. "Not the fender, not the fender."

The fender takes a crushing blow. My mom winces.

"Kill 'em, Ronnie, " our neighbors shout. "Kill 'em, boy."

Now I see an old Chevy that looks like my first car, my high school muscle car. I loved that car. It had a three twenty-seven engine, Holley carbs, headers jacked up past yer ass, and so much Bondo a magnet wouldn't stick anywhere. That car could've made it past airport security.

Now the field is down to three cars: Ronnie, Jennie's Hair Design, and 3:16. 3:16 only has one working wheel and spins harmlessly in circles. I can see the driver's lips moving and he sure ain't praying. Ronnie decides to take out Jennie in Mom's Nova.

"Ronnie, get her in the radiator."

My mom yells, "No, come on, Jennie."

The family looks over at Mom. "Get her Ronnie, kill, kill."

My mom yells, "The strut, go for the rear strut."

The family can't believe my mom has betrayed them. My mom can't believe they have the gall to think they love their son more that she loves her car.

Finally, Ronnie delivers a blow to Jennie, and Mom's car goes silent. We hear the engine trying to restart, but no use. Ronnie methodically puts 3:16 out of his misery, and it's over. My mom is crushed. "My Nova," she repeats. "I loved that car."

We decide to leave before the second round of competition. As we exit, I look at the new combatants, but it's the same cars. Ronnie, Jennie, and 3:16 are up and running. No, this isn't right, I think. It's like Mercutio returning in the fourth act of *Romeo and Juliet*. I'm even more upset that the mechanics had them up and running so fast. My own garage takes over a week for a simple rattle, and my mechanic has a bald spot on the side of his head from scratching it over my engine.

As we exit, I look at Mom. Now there is a fire in her eye. That look in someone's eye whose life will never be the same. Something tells me we'll be in those stands again this year, come Fourth of July. Look out, Ronnie.

State Fair

ONE SUMMER my friend Ted came to visit from Holland. I met him in Europe while I was performing with a circus, and now he was coming to work as a clown with a local theater troupe. When he arrived, the U.S. government gave him a pamphlet titled "Why Americans Act That Way." It was full of descriptions of idiosyncrasies and habits Americans have that most other countries do not share. I thought we were pretty much in step with everyone else. Then Ted read aloud some of our "special traits," and I was surprised to learn some of them were considered eccentric.

"Americans believe change is good."

I said, "Yeah, of course, change is good."

"No," he said, "it's not. In most of da rest of de world, change could mean a coup, or a flood. No, change is bad."

I said, "Or it could mean winning the lottery, or finding gold in the sewers."

"Gold in the sewers?"

"Don't tell me you've never gone into the sewers looking for gold?"

"No."

"Man, you just gave me an idea."

Ted said, "Let me read anudder one. 'Americans don't believe in fate.'"

"Like what, a palm reader?"

"No," he said. "Fate. Surely you must believe in fate. There is a plan, already in action, and we are playing it out."

"That's crazy. We determine the future."

"No, we don't. You think you control your future?"

"Of course, or why get up in the morning? How do accomplish anything? Why play sports, if it's already determined? No wonder you don't like football."

"I do like futball."

"I mean real football, with pads and helmets and cheerleaders."

"I like our futball, yours is too violent, and the fact we believe in fate does not mean we don't enchoy seeing it happen. In fact, dere is a comfort in knowing dere is a plan."

"Not for me. I like it when life is a surprise, one I can control."

"Finding gold in sewers."

"That's right," I said. "Hey, I know what we . . ."

"No," he said.

"No, I have another idea. Come on. We're going to the State Fair."

His eyes narrowed. "What is dis Shtate Fair?"

The State Fair. Seriously, you'll thank me later.

We hop in the car and drive from Minneapolis to St. Paul. It's right next door, the first city of the East, steeped in tradition like all those eastern cities: Beantown, Philly, the Big Apple (or, as my buddy calls it, "Sondheim and Gomorrah"). We're brothers, Twin Cities born at different times.

Ted and I arrive at the fairgrounds and it's a madhouse. Thousands of people from all over the state have come to attend. It's the end of summer, Labor Day, and we're all taking a break from work to check out the old favorites and the new foods. There's a huge traffic jam. "Okay," I say, "first thing is, we need a place to park."

Ted says, "Dere's a parking lot. And it appears to be quite empty."

"No, Ted, you can't park in the lot. It just isn't done."

"But it is only five dollars."

"Not doing it, Ted, at the Fair you park on the street. Tradition."

Ted and I drive around the block in an ever-widening search for a spot. After a half an hour, Ted is agitated, but I know he'll feel the euphoria of free parking once we find it.

I'm reminded of a story about an Irish guy who is late for a meeting. He's looking for a parking place, but all the meters are taken. He drives around the block but has no luck. Now he's really late. Out of frustration, he prays to God, "God, please, please help me find a parking place. Please, Lord, I'll stop my evil ways, put down the bottle, cease my philandering. Please, God, just help me find a parking spot." All of a sudden an open space appears. The man says, "Never mind, God, I found one."

Ted says, "Dat is a Belgian joke."

"No, it's not, Ted, it's Irish."

"Why Irish?"

"I don't know, just is. Why Belgian?"

"I don't know."

"Hey, a spot."

There's a place. I'm sort of in front of a fire hydrant and blocking a driveway, but it's not bad. Besides, we're only about a mile from the Fair. This is incredible luck, I tell Ted.

For some reason he can't forget that parking lot.

We walk to the main entrance of the fairgrounds. A thirty-foot fiberglass statue of a gopher welcomes everyone, a beautifully rendered representation of our state mascot in a suit and tie: Goldie the Gopher.

Ted says, "Why a gopher?"

"I don't know. Why not?"

"A gopher, dis is a rodent, vermin. Cows break der legs in der holes. Dey are poisoned, hated by your farmers."

"We love Goldie. And he's a thirteen-striped ground squirrel."

"Why is he called Goldie?"

All of a sudden I realize there's a lot I don't know. I've never questioned Goldie as our mascot. Huge, powerful, über-gopher with bulging biceps and a buck-toothed grin. What better representative?

As Ted rants about gophers I can see some people looking at him in building anger. This could turn sour. I better defuse the situation.

To calm him down, I say, "You see, Ted, in this country, we believe in change. And yes, there's even hope for the gopher. That one day he'll mend his ways and live in harmony with the farmer. This here's an homage to his resiliency in this effort and his coming over to our ways." My eyebrows go up and down, informing him there's more to my argument than my argument.

Ted says, "I see," but he's not buying it. Me neither.

We get inside and are met with a sea of "my people" and the smell of cooking grease, the reason they look the way they do. We are a large people. In the old days, we needed our weight to survive. With long fasts, famines, one's body needed to build reserves. Skinny people died. Now, the faminc lasts from breakfast to the coffee break. Not a lot of time to live off the reserves.

Folks are milling about. Many couples share similar themed T-shirts, with sayings like "I'm with Stupid" and an arrow pointing to the side. Some are already drinking from small Pepto-Bismol bottles. Lots of kids in strollers. Junior high kids in mortal terror someone will catch them having a good time with, heaven forbid, their parents. They are biding time to break free into the Midway, where there are more of their kind.

First, Machinery Hill.

My dad used to love going to Machinery Hill. In fact, the first five years I went to the State Fair, I thought that was all there was. The first year I stepped off "the Hill" into the Midway, it was like entering Oz.

I show Ted a plaque that lists the name of farmers whose farms date back a hundred years. Ted says his farm at home goes back to 1066, to William the Conqueror.

I say, "Bet he never had one of these."

I hop up into a John Deere combine. It's enormous, with an enclosed cab, stereo system, cup holders. State-of-the-art machinery.

"No," says Ted. "Dis ting is obscene."

"Yep," I say with a huge grin.

My dad would've been all over this thing, exclaiming, "Well, I'll be darned," or just "I'll be," at least a hundred times, getting the back of his shirt all grass stained. That's how you can tell the farmers at the fair. The backs of their shirts are grass stained from crawling under all the machinery.

I turn to Ted. "How's about we watch a calf being born, and then grab something to eat?"

On the way to the barns, we pass by the talent tent. There are country time cloggers in calico dancing to "In the Mood," followed by a quartet of young girls, sisters in taffeta dresses, singing, "Wasting away again in Margaritaville, searching for my lost shaker of salt" and enunciating every syllable to perfection.

To me, this is paradise.

We hit the birthing barn. Like Ted, the little calf isn't too sure about coming to the Fair. Finally, with one big pull, the little guy is out. The small crowd cheers.

Ted feels some things should be done in private.

WE WALK BACK to the food building. It is battered and deep fried.

Ted's on a roll.

"You call dis beer?"

"You call dis a sausage?"

"You call dis cheese?"

"Come on, Ted." I try to instruct him. "This kind of beer is designed to quench your thirst after mowing the lawn. It goes down fast, ice cold and smooth. The only reason you guys like warm beer is because of your poor refrigeration.

"And it's not sausage, it's a hot dog. Or a footlong. Say sausage to one of these vendors and they'll stare at you, like you just said, 'Please stare at me blankly.'

"And these are cheese curds. Fresh cheese. So fresh they should squeak on your teeth when you bite them."

"We age our cheese to perfection."

"The perfect age for this cheese is twenty minutes. Get used to it, Ted. Let's get some roasted corn."

"Corn? We call dis maize. We feed it to our pigs. I will not eat pig food."

"Your loss, Ted."

He did eat the fried cheese curds, though. And thank goodness he didn't try to convince me that cheese came from Europe. He'd already tried to tell me the fiddle and guitar came from there. I don't know what their schools teach them, but I'm glad he's here, where he can learn. I think it would be good for more Europeans to travel. Learn what the world is really like.

Now it's time for "All the milk you can drink for a quarter." Ted says, "Milk is what we give the children."

"Come on, Ted, nothing cuts the grease like a cold paper cup or ten of milk." I start in drinking. Meanwhile Ted goes into the dairy building and watches a woman sculpt one of the Dairy Princesses out of a huge block of butter. The Princess and the sculptor wear coats and are stationed in a refrigerated glass booth. I stand at the milk counter 'til I feel I've drunk my money's worth.

When I find Ted he's still staring at the booth like it's an alien from *Close Encounters of the Third Kind*.

"Come on, Ted. Now the fun begins. We're going to the Midway."

"Midway?"

"Rides."

"Dere is a ride." Ted points to a building with small boats running into a channel and a large wheel churning in the water.

"No, Ted, that's Ye Olde Mill."

"It looks gentle."

"It is. It's a boat ride that goes through dark tunnels. Every once in a while a very . . . uh, unique diorama will appear. One has plaster deer and raccoon statues, another has gnomes making shoes. One has outer space people and Knights of the Round Table."

"Sounds good."

I explain to Ted in a whisper. "Okay, Ted. We are a people that are slow to boil. But I figure back somewhere in our distant past, maybe through Viking raids, we acquired a recessive Latin gene, an unexplained phenomenon that has made us prone to sudden and unexpected acts of passion. You never know when this recessive gene will flare up. This ride is here just in case, while you're at the Fair with your date, that Latin gene kicks in. You can take a quick cruise and reset the levels in private."

Ted is staring at me like I am in the Butter Princess booth, with a mixture of belief and disbelief. Finally Ted says he doesn't even want to imagine this crowd "resetting their levels," so we take a pass on Ye Olde Mill.

We enter the Midway, stepping over huge electric cables running to rides. Junior high kids run free of parents. It reminds me of where Pinocchio ends up just before turning into a donkey.

Ted wants to go on the Ferris wheel, but I say, "No, that's for wimps," and talk him into a ride that will be forever known as "the return of the corndog."

After apologies all around, we walk past the blue whale truck. A loudspeaker blares, "If it isn't real, you can keep the truck."

I told Ted, don't even think about it. "I've wasted a lot of money in there. They won't give you the truck."

We continue along the rows of rides and games. Barkers try to get our attention.

Ted stops. "What is dis?"

"It's an old-time freak show."

A man stands out front of the tent. "See the amazing Popeye, the Sword Swallower, and Ape Lady, found in the wilds of the Amazon, descended from the lost species, *Orangutangus maximus,* the missing link."

Ted says, "I would like to see dis missing link."

"Are you sure, Ted?"

"Yes. It is important."

"All right." I mean, it's the first thing he's wanted to do.

We go into the tent. The sword swallower looks like swords were the only thing he has ever swallowed. Gaunt, thin, white as a sheet, but he manages to slide down some impressive hardware.

"Come on," says Ted.

We go to the next tent. "Popeye." A man who can pop his eyes out of his head. I remember a lot of kids from junior high who ended up in the nurse's office because of this guy.

Popeye enters, and Ted says, "It's de same guy. Dat's de sword swallower."

It was. Same guy, now in a turban and cape.

Shhhh, somebody says.

We go into the next tent. "Gorilla Lady," a woman who turns into a gorilla. Ted says it better not be the sword swallower. It isn't. A woman enters: dark hair, bikini with gold tassels, a stare that certainly once held mystery. A bright light hit us in the eyes, and there's a deafening roar. Before we can refocus, an ape stands before us, about the same height as the sword swallower, the thinnest ape I've ever seen.

The taped voice calls her "The Missing Link."

This set Ted off completely. Not that it was an obvious rip-off, but that they dared to tell us this is the missing link. Ted says, "Missing link to what? To us? To people? Dey can't tell us dis."

Now I remember why *Close Encounters of the Third Kind* was a tragedy for Ted. Ted stared at the screen long after the movie had ended. Then he said, "Dis cannot be. How do dey dare tell us what aliens will look like? Dis is a crime." A nervous usher said he could have his money back, but Ted said, "I don't want my money back, dey must stop showing dis. Tink of de children." We were told we couldn't go back there anymore, and I believed them.

He has the same look about him now. I decide to get Ted out of the Midway before he shouts, "Tink of de children." This place is designed to escalate instability—the lights, blaring rock music. Ted was going to blow.

A teenager screams and beats his chest after knocking over a milk bottle with a ball. His girlfriend gets a large orange stuffed dog.

Ted says, "Dere. *Dat* is de missing link."

We're almost to the Midway exit when I hear a voice, a voice like no other, a voice on its last vocal cord. Raw from screaming, but through sheer will still audible and direct.

"Hey. Hey, you!"

Everything in me says don't turn, don't turn, but like Orpheus exiting hell, I can't resist, I have to know. I turn.

And there he sits . . . the dunking clown.

The dunking clown is a man dressed as a clown sitting in an enclosed booth. He's perched approximately ten feet off the ground on a small platform over a tank of water five feet deep. On one side of the tank is a wooden arm that extends from under his seat, outside the confines of the booth, with a target painted on its end. The goal of the clown is to insult passersby until, from rage or ego, the patron purchases the use of three balls to be tossed at the target. If one hits the target, the arm pulls from under the seat and the clown drops into the water.

The clown wears bad makeup and the condition of the

water appears far from hygienic. By all rights, it should be ignored. But I remember this guy. He's been doing this since I was a kid. He's amazing. He berates, goads, chides, embarrasses, harasses. His arsenal of insults knows no limits. He could get Gandhi to throw a ball. He's that good.

I intentionally try to walk Ted past the dunk tank, his last nerve as threadbare as the clown's last vocal cord. But the clown sees Ted.

"Hey, hey, you two wimpy turds."

Ted's politeness gets the best of him.

"Ja," says Ted. "What is it you want?"

And the clown has him.

"Yeah. Yeah, you. What's the matter, don't you like me? Hey!"

"I like you chust fine."

The clown starts in. "Come on, are you a Kraut?"

"I am from Holland."

"We pulled your ass out of the war."

"You should not speak."

"Oh, I'll speak. I'll speak."

The clown strategy is to get guys so enraged they can't throw straight. They throw too hard. I've seen more than one irate patron dismiss the target entirely and try to hit the clown directly through the chicken wire that protects him.

What he doesn't know is that Ted is a clown purist. Actually one of the best performers I have ever seen. This guy is wearing the face paint of a clown that should never speak. Between the ape lady and this disregard for one of the things he holds most sacred, Ted has gone beyond endurable limits.

Ted says something in Dutch that seemed to require even more phlegm than usual.

He then pays for three balls.

The clown is laughing, singing "Lili Marleen."

Ted holds the ball over his head, soccer style.

This send the clown into hysterics.

The ball misses. Ted says, "Opebakkus." It's a Flemish word. I don't know what it means but the only guy I ever heard use it in Belgium got punched in the nose.

The second toss misses as well.

"Hey, turd," yells the clown, "is that your name?"

"My name is . . . Ted."

The third ball hits the target and the clown drops into the filthy water.

The crowd cheers.

Ted rushes the glass and pounds on it.

"Take dat, shtupid little man. Dat's for you."

Okay, now I really have to get him out of here. This could escalate into a serious clown fight.

Ted is tanked up on cheese curds and he just kicked some clown ass. He now feels good about himself.

I TAKE HIM TO THE horticulture building. We watch honeybees dance in a hive to inform the others where to find the clover. It seems to soothe Ted. He still thinks he should report that clown for wearing improper makeup.

We then look at the crop art. These are artworks made

entirely by gluing seeds of different shapes and colors to a board. It's a lot like three-dimensional paint-by-numbers. For some reason, the crop art people are a very leftist bunch. Che Guevara, Fidel Castro, Louis Armstrong, Eleanor Roosevelt are all immortalized, unless they get watered, in seed. Ted takes comfort in this as well.

We watch a man selling knives. He announces that with each purchase, one gets a juicer, six steak knives, and a dicer. The demonstration includes "vege-gami," a cucumber carved into a fish, a radish into a rose, a watermelon into a cityscape with seeds acting as windows of the tenements. Then we witness a knife sawing through a twelve-penny nail, a tin can, and a two-by-four board, then he uses the very same knife to cut paper-thin tomato slices. Ted decides to buy a knife. I tell him wait and buy the second set—the hawker had used the first set to cut through that nail.

I'm glad we saw the ape woman before the knives.

Then we're off to the poultry barn to see what the fancy chickens are wearing this year. Their fashion heights are matched only by their attitudes. Divas all, but beautiful.

By some great fortune, the display of grand pianos is placed in the hog barn and we are treated to a sonata while gazing at the "world's largest hog."

Finally, we end up in the llama barn. It's competition day to determine the prize llama. Llamas are often kept with sheep because they will defend a flock from coyotes and even wolves. They are supposedly as stubborn as mules, and we witness this firsthand. The llamas are first to run an obstacle course. It is designed to aggravate more than to test dexterity. Stepping over a "wall" maybe five inches high doesn't appear that difficult, but to a llama this is more a matter of pride. The handlers pull the reins, but because their necks are so long, the llamas simply bend their heads forward, their feet remaining firmly planted. Few make it past the wall, even fewer beyond the kiddie pool, and only two finish the course entirely.

Next is a fashion show, with the llamas wearing sweaters knitted from their own wool. I think Ted will have a fit, but he seems to enjoy the designs. One reminds him of a sweater his Norwegian grandmother had made him. Finally, the last event: the costume parade.

The third place winner is announced first, a llama dressed in authentic Peruvian attire. The handler, a boy of about twelve, is also decked out in the Andean style of dress.

"Very nice," says Ted.

"Pretty lame," says the guy in front of us.

Second place goes to a duo sporting a Dutch theme. Ted seems a bit embarrassed. He says, "Oh, no." The girl is dressed as a little Dutch girl, with blonde pigtails, a blue dress and apron, and wooden shoes. She dances to what sounds like Bavarian yodeling. The llama wears a nice Dutch boy hat, shirt and tie, and lederhosen, but the real showstoppers are the two windmills spinning at his sides. The audience applauds wildly. Ted is holding his head in his hands, possibly overwhelmed with pride in his country.

Then the lights dim. As first place is announced, music blares from the speakers and spotlights hit the star attraction: Batman and Robin. Yes, the Caped Crusader and Boy

Wonder. The "boy" is actually a girl dressed as Robin, side-kick to the Gotham crime fighter. The llama has blue taffeta cowling on its head, complete with ears and eye slots, a neck piece running the entire length of its neck, black tights adorning its spindly front legs, and a cape stretched across its back. But most impressive are the fake arms attached at its shoulders, held outstretched in front of its body, giving an illusion of flight. The crowd goes nuts. The llama is looking around, calmly chewing whatever it is chewing, as Robin nimbly dances around his mentor. Batman, in the smallest tights I have ever seen, "flies" across the arena. It is spectacular.

Ted whispers, "Unbelievable. I am amazed at dis. Truly."

The guy in front of us tells Ted, "You should've seen last year. The winner was dressed like Kirby Puckett, center fielder for the Minnesota Twins. He had arms attached, too, with huge muscles, and a baseball bat. This Batman is pretty good, though."

That's when I think I hear something snap in Ted. Way deep.

"Dese llamas are brilliant, really. An art form unto demselves."

The argumentative Ted is gone. We leave the llama barn.

He eats corn, pays a dollar to have a guy guess his weight, even makes a recording in the karaoke booth. "Dere is a huis in New Orleans, dey call de Rising Sun. It's been de ruin of many a poor boy, und Gott, I hope I'm one."

For a while he sleeps on a bench in front of the talent tent as a baton twirler dances to the theme song from

Rocky. Snoozing away in his mustard-stained shirt, with his free yardstick between his knees, he looks like a happy Dutchman on a stick.

I sneak off to try to find an "I'm with Stupid" T-shirt to give him if we come back next year.

When he wakes, we walk to the main entrance. On the way out, he says, "Bye-bye, Goldie."

I am so proud. Holding that corndog, with his blank expression and that smile plastered on his face, he could've been a Minnesotan.

"C'mon, Ted, let's go."

"Okay."

While I've got him in this mood, I'll swing over to the gas station and buy some lottery tickets. Then can we look for gold.

But first, I have to remember where I parked that car.

Waiting for Mr. Mershing

WE MOVE TO THE COUNTRY when I am eight, and we have to take the bus to school. The Catholic kids sit up front and the public kids in the back. All the Catholic kids are let off at St. Francis Catholic School, and the rest of us walk a block and a half to the public school. On the way past St. Francis, I put my fingers through the chain-link fence and watch to see how the Catholic kids play. I notice they play a lot like us, but I know in that church they had other games, games like Catechism, some weird cross between catacombs and hypnotism. And the girls run about all in their plaid dresses and the boys in their blue shorts and white shirts. I wonder if when Halloween comes, they all have to be little plaid witches, and holy ghosts with short pants and white shirts.

Suddenly . . . *whap!* A ruler strikes my fingers through the fence.

"Nuns! Run for your lives, it's the Nuns!"

So when Halloween arrives and Mom asks me what I wanted to be, I pick the most frightening thing I can think of. I say, "A nun. I wanna be a nun."

"No," she says. "Kevin, nuns are peaceful, God-fearing people."

Was she brainwashed, or what?

"A monk? Then can I be a monk?"

"Yes, that's fine."

For some reason a monk was okay.

I wasn't that keen on being a monk. When selecting a Halloween costume, I always liked to choose what I feared most, in hopes of overcoming the terror by living inside the feared thing's skin. A monk didn't fit my criteria.

My brother always picked a costume to try out another way to exact vengeance on the human race. One year we both went as Richard Nixon.

Another year he went as the devil. The costume was a plastic mask and red suit from the drugstore. After he got the candy, he said, "Thank you. I'll see you in hell." He never said it like a threat, more like, "See ya later." Then he stood in the doorway; his happy little blue eyes peering from inside the mask. The effect was unnerving. Neighbors were calling for days wondering if Steven was mad at them for some reason, and whatever that reason was, they were sorry.

This year he is a Choctaw warrior. Mostly because he likes the word "Choctaw."

So, I am a reluctant monk, and my brother is a Choctaw

warrior, out for trick or treat. We are not happy. Now that we live in the country, there are only two houses within walking distance. About a block from our house, I turn and see my mom is nowhere in sight. I flip my hood around, pull up my white turtleneck with the hole cut in the throat, and presto chango, I am a nun. I laugh out a guttural "Ave Maria" and sing "Climb every mountain" and "Dominique, 'nique, 'nique." I have a ruler hidden in my sock. Look out world, now it's the nun and the Choctaw warrior.

We arrive at the first home and knock on the door. A woman comes to the door.

"Trick or treat."

"Oh, trick or treat. Well, look at you. What are you?"

My brother says something completely unintelligible, and then looks at me.

"He says he is a Choctaw warrior, you silly white woman," I translate.

"Heavens, and you?"

"A n-u-u-u-u-u-un, *hahahahaha*. Ave Maria!" I whip the ruler out of my sock and strike a pose.

She says, "What?"

"A nun."

"But nuns are peaceful, God-fearing creatures."

She was brainwashed, just like Mom.

Then this lady takes out a huge bowl of candy, dumps half of it into my bag and the other half into my brother's bag, and says, "It's so nice to have children in the area." She closes the door and she's gone. We've only been to one house and we have full bags of candy. We still have another house to go! The nun and the Choctaw warrior are now dancing down the street.

"Oh," my brother drops to his knees and cries, "we should have brought the UNICEF cans."

We next arrive at a dilapidated old farmhouse. All the lights are off and the windmill in the yard squeaks as it turns in the cold, gray wind. Spooky. I knock on the door. It opens, *crrreeeeaaaakkk,* and there, sitting in his front hallway, is Mr. Mershing. Mr. Mershing has pulled his La-Z-Boy recliner to the front door, and next to him is an end table, and on the end table are two jars of pickles. One jar is marked "edible." And the other is marked "Halloween."

"Yeessss?"

"Trick or trea . . ."

"Oh, trick or treat," says Mr. Mershing. "Well, do you boys like pickles?"

"We love pickles. We can eat a million pickles."

"Oh, you can eat a million pickles?"

"A million, more or less."

"Well, how about one of theeeeesse?" And Mr. Mershing takes the jar marked "Halloween," unscrews the rusty lid, reaches into the jar, pulls out a pickle, and sets it on the table. These are the largest and most unnaturally green pickles I have ever seen. Mr. Mershing hands one pickle to me and one to my brother, licks his fingers, and rasps, "There you go, boys, and you can have as many as you want, but you must eat them all in front of meeeeeeeeee."

No problem. My brother and I take our pickles, "Cheers," and start in.

I take a large bite, and . . . and . . . ahhhhh, it's so hot. Ahhhh, my eyes are watering, my forehead itches and I have a smile on my face, but not because I'm happy. It's because my cheek muscles are pinching so hard my lips are trying to crawl around the back of my head. My brother has a smile too, but he isn't happy either. I cough, wheeze, and finally choke down the rest of the pickle.

Mr. Mershing says, "Would you like another?"

"Of course we would. Pickles are supposed to hurt like this."

We eat pickle after pickle, Mr. Mershing laughing the whole time. At one point he joins in, chomping on a scary-looking gherkin and sweating and crying and choking right along with us.

And every Halloween we return to see who can eat the most Mershing pickles.

Then one year, Mr. Mershing stops handing out pickles. They're building a house where his garden used to be, another building where his house used to be. I ask my mom what happened to him. She tells me, "Kevin, Mr. Mershing was a farmer. He had lived in that house and worked that land his entire life, until the city started to move out here. Then his taxes rose so high Mr. Mershing couldn't afford his land anymore. And that's when they found him in his garage."

Had he killed himself? I didn't ask. I didn't want to know.

The next year my brother and I tote full bags of candy from the housing development that has sprung up in the area. At Mr. Mershing's farm, the house where his garden used to be is finished, and there is a new restaurant where the farmhouse used to be.

My brother and I sit in the restaurant parking lot. I say, "I wish Mr. Mershing were here."

My brother says, "Me, too. Maybe he is."

I ask him if he is afraid. He says, "No."

I'm not either. I know if there is a ghost it'll be Mr. Mershing. My brother reaches into his bag and pulls out a jar of pickles he's brought from home. "How about one of theeeeese?"

And we sit on the curb eating pickles, waiting for Mr. Mershing. I'm sure to anyone driving by, it just looked like two Richard Nixons sitting in a parking lot eating pickles.

The Goat

IN THE FALL OF 1974, I attended college in a small town in southern Minnesota. It was a sleepy campus. Occasionally, fraternities fell under Dionysus' weekend spell.

There were still a few Vietnam vets around, though, guys on the GI Bill who had seen and done things that left them permanently immune to authority, and there was a smattering of academics, artsy types, vegetarian free thinkers. The elite of this group called themselves the Brain Trust, inhalers as opposed to ingesters, who felt it their mission to bring down "The Man." They could be trouble.

After a horrific food fight in the cafeteria, they penned their famous "When buns are outlawed, only outlaws will have buns" manifesto for the school paper, which included an irrefutable argument: "Buns don't throw buns, people throw buns." The school administration was not amused. The angry youngster was, after all, a thing of the past.

At the time, I was a theater major, mostly because the only thing easier than a theater major was a theater minor. My subversive acts were limited to putting Mr. Yuck stickers on cafeteria trays and wearing socks with sandals because I knew the look put some people off.

That is, until the Brain Trust approached me with a project.

One of the school's professors, Dr. Kloss, taught surrealism, economics, and German, and he raised goats on a farm outside of town. One morning Dr. Kloss awoke to find several members of the Brain Trust and me on his farm.

"Yes, vat do you boys vant?"

"We'd like to buy a goat."

"Vat do you want vis zis goat for?" asked Dr. Kloss.

"To run for homecoming queen."

Dr. Kloss loved homecoming, a celebration like a small Oktoberfest. It was why he could live in America. He loved to drink and sing and dance.

But he loved surrealism more, and that Something with a cloven hoof should represent the student body thrilled him to the marrow.

"I only haff a ram for sale."

"That's fine."

"Could he vin?"

"We think so, Dr. Kloss."

Now Herschel wasn't much to look at. Even for a goat, he was one of the more unattractive creatures on the planet—more like a small buffalo. One of the Brain Trust remarked, "No one in their right mind would sleep with that goat," and it was true. And he smelled horrible. It simply took your breath away, and Dr. Kloss confessed that no amount of soap would help. Herschel may have also been the most amorous creature on the planet. As learned on the ride home, gender was of no importance to him, nor species, nor animal-mineral-or-vegetable, for that matter. And it was later learned that he could hold his alcohol, and in fact inhale. In no time, Herschel fit right in.

Now, to get him elected. This is where I came into play.

Talent was out. Looks were out. He would have to work on his platform. To do that, someone would have to voice the goat's opinions. The Brain Trust knew I had an interest in the theatrical arts and wondered if I would provide the proper voice for Herschel. I told them my vocal range was a bit high, not distinguished enough for the task. However, there was one man for the job: a student actor, Rick Richards, the self-proclaimed love child of Liberace and Rock Hudson, the only man in the Midwest who said "Broad-WAY" and "Waiting for GOD-ot." And called Sir Lawrence Olivier "Larry."

Rick always wore an ascot and smoked a pipe, and at any given moment he would drop into that B-movie East Coast British accent like Katharine Hepburn, even though he came from Illinois. "Or Illinwa. Rally, I did."

I was in a production of *Bus Stop* with Rick. He decided his character, the sheriff, should have a limp. For the benefit of the audience, and to show his professionalism, Rick managed always to limp on the downstage leg. Amazing. I reminded Rick that every great performer was linked to an animal, in one way or another, on the ladder to stardom.

After a lengthy pause in which he seemed focused on a mythic horizon, he took his pipe from his lips and agreed to provide Herschel's voice.

On meet-the-candidates night, the auditorium was packed. Most students came to laugh or jeer. A familiar lineup of cheerleaders and sorority sisters filed across the stage. Then Herschel walked into the spotlight. Silence. He scanned the room with those insane goat eyes, then began to speak. "My fellow students, lend me your ears."

He addressed the outsiders, those who don't fit in. He assured them they now had a voice. At once, he was Julius Caesar, the Music Man, and Henry Higgins, calling the audience Romans, Iowans, and gov'nas. He was Juliet crying out for love in the night, Mad Ophelia, Carmen, Ethel Merman belting, "I don't know how to love him." Rick then applied an old vaudeville trick. Any hoofer in a chorus line knows if you repeat a step seven times the audience will automatically applaud. Kick seven times—applause. Herschel repeated, "I feel your pain" seven times until . . .

The audience leapt to its feet as one. Wild, raucous adulation. Herschel was an instant celebrity.

Men found him virile. His sensitivity and musky smell proved irresistible to women. And the vets loved his blatant disregard for the campus foliage.

He rode triumphantly on the homecoming royalty float dressed as a southern belle amid a crepe paper plantation. A football player dressed as Rhett Butler had to restrain his date only once, when Dr. Kloss appeared, weeping and waving from the crowd.

The election of Herschel brought a calming effect on the campus. The students had been heard, and subversive acts all but stopped.

Then came the ribbon cuttings, the charity events, the state pageant where Herschel competed, unsuccessfully, with other queens from throughout Minnesota. For months Herschel was everywhere, attending parties, school functions, arguing for better food, a new theater facility, even finding time to pen a weekly opinion column for the paper: "Get My Goat."

Yet as the year rolled into winter and toward spring, he and Rick slowly fell out of synch. Herschel still appeared at his required functions, but sometimes his speeches were mere lines read from upcoming school productions or long passages of biology text. The Brain Trust was already off on another project to topple The Man, this one involving a large phallic structure and the statue of the Jolly Green Giant just north of town. Herschel's enthusiasm waned as well, except for trips to nursing homes and hospitals. No one there seemed to mind his odor. They patted his bony head and didn't expect him to save the world. Finally his reign came to an unceremonious conclusion.

At the end of the year, it seemed cruel to return Herschel to farm life. He wasn't really a goat anymore. Didn't find other goats attractive, only liked campus food. So an ad was placed in the paper. If you ever want to see a truly frightening cross section of humanity, put a "goat/homecoming queen for sale" ad in the newspaper. We eventually gave him back to Dr. Kloss. And that was the last I saw of Herschel.

Rick graduated to play in a community production of *GodSPELL* and to appear in waterbed warehouse commercials. The great Brain Trust graduated and went on to work for corporations or the government. The vets still buck authority. I went back to wearing socks with sandals.

I REMEMBER LEAVING Herschel on the farm. He stood and stared at us as we got into the car. He seemed sad. Then he saw Dr. Kloss and gave a little leap in the air. Herschel was home, the bright lights and life in the fast lane already a fading memory. I could see Dr. Kloss petting Herschel's head, then smell his hand and make a face.

As long as I live, I will never forget how Herschel stood before an audience, paused, and simply stared with those insane eyes scanning the room. And for a moment, just a moment, the goat held us, all on his own. Then he would begin. "My fellow students. . . ." God bless America.

Vets

MY BROTHER AND I LIKED to play army man out in the backyard behind the garage of my grandparents' house. During one Christmas visit, the small green plastic men are surrounded by an enemy force of blue Knights of the Round Table, yellow Hessians, and some gray plastic unknown army that was just always "the enemy." Things look bad for the army men. Supplies are running low, almost out of ammo, no reinforcements available, the box is empty.

One young recruit says, "I don't think we're going to make it, Sarge."

"Don't worry, son," says the sergeant. "I've seen worse." But things do look bad for the army men.

Suddenly my brother says, "Wait!" He runs into the house and comes out with the two-inch pink Baby Jesus from my grandmother's manger scene. Brilliant. We know the power of the Baby Jesus, we learned it on the school playground from Mary Marhoula, a Catholic and therefore an expert. According to Mary, nothing could harm the Baby Jesus because his Father, God, needed him to grow up to become sacrificed.

The Baby Jesus is carried to the army men by a one-legged G.I. Joe who says, "I've had worse," and dies. We promise him a Viking funeral later in the day, if we can find some lighter fluid.

The Hessians shout, "Give yourselves up!"

The young recruit answers, "Don't make the Baby Jesus come over there."

The Hessians shout, "Who sayeth he is the Son of God?"

The Baby Jesus stands. "I sayeth."

He's met with a volley of bullets, but they bounce off his chest like marshmallows. A lot like marshmallows.

The Hessians devise an "A-bomb," a cinder block, eight by twelve by sixteen inches, from behind the garage. The A-bomb hovers briefly over the Baby Jesus and drops. The Hessians go off rejoicing, to worship idols and eat forbidden fruit.

Minutes, what seems like an eternity goes by, then the A-bomb begins to move, then to shake, then magically lifts up to reveal an unharmed Baby Jesus. Gonna now give them Hessians a little taste of the Old Testament.

The Hessians, in their ignorant fear, cower in a perfect eight-by-sixteen-inch formation. The A-bomb hovers over them briefly, miraculously, then drops on those who "lived by the sword."

We go into the house for leftovers and gently return the

Baby Jesus to the manger scene, where he quietly goes back to civilian life and his day job saving the souls of mankind.

THIS WAS MY VIEW OF WAR: comic book heroes, daring stories, great warring nations: Spartans, Vikings, Apaches, Ninjas, Cossacks, Romans, Amazons. Legends and heroes greater than mere mortals, all with their own gods of war.

History is written by the winners: His Story. There was a glamour and glory around combat.

Later I would read the speeches of Herodotus, Lincoln, and Roosevelt, and Shakespeare's *Henry the Fifth*—words that would get the blood to boil. I knew the incredible music of war: bagpipes, marches, drums and bugles, George M. Cohan, the Andrews Sisters, rock and roll, folk music—all arrive at times of conflict.

ULTIMATELY, HOWEVER, the fighting has been done by individuals. For some, it started as an adventure or a step into adulthood. For most, this task was not a natural act but a duty to be endured.

I've been surprised to hear about positive experiences from those I know who have served. My buddy Joe, a Vietnam vet, speaks of the green and the beauty of driving through a field one day in country. He gets a look of serenity that seems like it can't be associated to the danger he was in, but that's what he was feeling. There are times, he says, when through the boredom or foul weather or homesickness, something happens. Something simple—dry socks, a letter, a hot meal, a very small gesture—is magnified and becomes a reminder of how beautiful life can be . . . in perspective. When he's with other vets, they laugh. The humor is bent and dark, and only those who were there can laugh.

For some of my friends who returned from all the intensity of that war, the pace of everyday life just doesn't seem to come up to snuff. They tend to drive fast.

MY UNCLE, THE ONE who served in World War II, laughed and joked with my dad and his brothers, but I noticed when he got quiet, he got a deep quiet. I envied this knowledge but wondered how he acquired it. I realized he had seen and done things that few will ever know.

For everyone returning after the conflict, there is the reentry to civilian life, a life that has moved on without them. For some it's a gentle step. For others, like Odysseus returning from Battle of Troy, another battle ensues, trying to fit in with what he now knows, who he has become, even his wife not recognizing him. Where do you begin the rebuilding? What unwelcome memories return with you? My uncle's wife has an experience of war as well, without having ever left the country. I can see her watching him in ways other wives do not. Their love knows a terrain, levels uncharted and deep.

I know that knowledge isn't cheap. My uncle's deep solitude came at a price, and there are truths I could recognize but will probably never know. I do know that at some point in life, he made a choice, perhaps because of his allegiance to God, country, or family, and for that he would risk life and limb. That choice is related to me, and I am connected and indebted to him.

ANOTHER CHRISTMAS in the early 1980s. I'm in London, flat broke and missing my family. I decide to see a play as a treat and to take my mind off the terrible time I imagine they're having without me. How can they laugh and enjoy themselves with me not there? I walk to the West End and plunk down my last two pounds, about four dollars, to sit up in the nosebleed section. The play is *The Dresser,* staring Tom Courtenay and Albert Finney. The action takes place backstage in a London theater during World War II. An aging actor, his dresser, and a town of misfits try to perform a play while air raid sirens blare and bombs rain down. The play is really about the relationship of these two men and the bonds created through triumph and adversity.

An elderly couple sits next to me, and occasionally they lift their glasses and wipe their eyes. I wonder if they lived through the devastation depicted in the play. At intermission, the man tells me he fought in World War II. This play brings back a lot of memories for both him and his wife.

The play is also full of songs. As the second act begins, an old phonograph plays "A Nightingale Sang in Barkley Square." The man takes my hand in his and sings along. In fact, the entire audience joins hands and sings along, swaying to the music. Me too, without really knowing the words. After the song ends, the man continues to hold my hand. During some of the next scenes, the bombing of London, he squeezes a little. Then another song begins, and his grip loosens.

Grace

THANKSGIVING IS A BIG HOLIDAY in my family. Before the meal we always bowed our heads in prayer. In my family it was called "saying grace." A time to pause and reflect on our good fortune, to say aloud we missed someone who couldn't be with us, to bless those who were there. It was a purposeful reaching to the sacred, time spent with "grace," that brief sensation we feel when in contact with the divine.

WHEN I WAS A KID, I loved visiting my grandparents' farm. We had lots of unstructured time. Now, they call it boredom, but I was never bored. I have never been bored. Sure, I've sat through some plays where I've wanted to be somewhere else and a few shows where I would've fallen asleep if I hadn't been the one talking, but I have never been bored.

I thank my Grandma Kling. My grandma taught me the beauty in the mundane.

Her name was Grace. She was the grandparent I felt furthest from, growing up. While my other grandmother was ample and smelled like cookie dough, Grandma Kling was frail and thin and smelled like frail and thin. There was always a little fear surrounding her. She ran their farmhouse in that systematic Germanic way that would've made her ancestors proud.

Above her stove was a cross-stitched plaque that read, "*Rein geht gut . . . komme besser raus.*"

"Go in good . . . come out better."

No truer words were ever stitched. Grandma's kitchen was an artist's studio, and whatever my grandpa provided as a medium, in a gesture she transformed, teased, poached, or pickled.

"If you leave here hungry, it's your own fault."

Pickled everything.

"If you don't see it on the table, you don't need it."

If Grandpa could cut it off, Grandma could pickle it.

"Don't ask for what you don't see, it's good training for later in life."

Grandma spoke as if she were always inventing another cross-stitching to hang over part of your life.

"Desires of any kind lead to nothing but trouble."

She ran a tight ship.

With livelihoods relying on fickle weather, crop selection, and market values, faith plays a large role in farmers' lives. Every Sunday found them in church. No one missed church for any reason. If you skipped for a fractured leg, it had better be compound.

It was during a sermon at my grandparents' church I heard a phrase that would forever change my life. While quoting Genesis, the pastor said that God said, "Thou shalt have no other gods before me."

This gave me pause. What a curious thing for God to blurt out.

In Sunday school, as I worked on a Play-Doh topographic representation of the Holy Land, I reflected on that sentence. If God said, "Thou shall have no other gods before me," then there clearly were other gods. God said so. God doesn't lie. I believed that. Why would he? Nobody could beat up God. Just to make sure I asked the Sunday school teacher.

"Mrs. Walker, can Jesus' dad beat up Buddha?"

"Yes, Kevin, Jesus' dad can beat up Buddha."

"Can Jesus' dad beat up Allah?"

"Yes, Kevin, Jesus' dad can beat up Allah."

"Can Jesus' dad beat up Odin?"

"Well now that's a tough fight, but yes, Kevin, Jesus' dad can beat up Odin."

I tasted the dough. Mmmm, salty. Not as good as public school dough, but pretty good. So if God said there were other gods, then there were other gods. Gods of love, hate, color, and song. Gods that lived in words, in places, in deeds.

But the true god, God God, was in charge of them all. This meant God was capable of, no, *required* to maintain complexities. This thought stunned me. God is complex. Where would it end? How far could this go?

I heard the Sunday school teacher's voice.

"Kevin, Kevin Kling."

"Yes, Miss Walker?"

"What are you doing?"

"What?"

"Your lips. Your lips."

A bluish-green outlined my lips.

And when I looked down at the Holy Land, I noticed I'd eaten over half of the Fertile Crescent.

But now it occurred to me if the great patriarch could be complex, so could the great matriarch, Grandma.

MY GRANDMA'S FAVORITE THING to do was to drive into Brookfield, Missouri, a town of about five thousand, and sit in her car at an angle parked on Main Street. This town always smelled like tractor grease. It seemed like it was always windy, and there was always a different three-legged dog running around. But through my grandma's eyes, it contained a world of wonder.

Grandma liked to keep a running commentary. Her favorite place to park was in front of the drugstore because you can tell a lot about someone by what they bring out of a drugstore.

"Look," Grandma said. Around the corner came a man, head down in concentration. As he walked past I could see his lips move. Grandma explains, "He counts his steps, every step of the day. He was in the war." Which war I don't know. Grandma said she went to grammar school with him. He used to pull her hair. Now look at him. She stares. Grandma had no problem with staring at people.

A woman walks past. As she walks, she develops a sudden hitch in her step. Then we watch as her drawers slip from under her dress and fall to the ground. In one beautiful fluid motion, she catches them on the toe of her shoe and kicks them into the air. The drawers do a one-and-a-half flip into her waiting pocketbook. It is incredible. Without missing a beat, Grandma says, "I would've left them."

"Why is that yellow car there?" She points to a parked yellow car. "Whose car is that?"

"I don't know, Grandma."

"Why is that there? Whose is that? . . . Oh, look," she says. "That restaurant closed. It opened on the day of a funeral. Who would have a mind to do such a thing? Kevin, never open a restaurant on the day of a funeral."

"All right, Grandma."

All of a sudden she sees one of her friends.

Grandma rolls down the window.

"Charlene, Charlene."

"Oh, hello, Grace. What brings you to town?"

"It's my hair day."

"Yes, that's right. Well, isn't that nice."

"Yes."

"Say, Grace, who owns that yellow car?"

"Well, I don't know."

"I don't either."

"Well."

"I know, honey, I know."

"All right, Charlene."

"All right, Grace."

The man who counts steps walks by, and now I can see his lips move. ". . . 5,067, 5,068, 5,069 . . ."

Suddenly Grandma says, "Don't look."

I look.

Grandma says, "That woman. She spits."

She points to an elderly woman in blue jeans. Now I don't mean to brag, but at age ten I considered myself somewhat of a spitting expert, known on the playground for distance and accuracy. But this woman launched a stream that seemed to do her bidding even in mid flight. It went around a fire hydrant before striking a paper cup. Then she shot me a look and smiled.

"Disgusting," Grandma says. "Kevin, Kevin, never fall for a woman who spits."

"All right, Grandma." But Grandma was so too late on this one.

Another of Grandma's rules was "No dogs in the house."

"It can't live outside, Grandma. It's a wiener dog. It will die."

She allowed this one exception. But one accident, and that was it. Outside.

It would have been, too. You didn't mess with Grandma.

We all knew how Grandma felt about the dog. Yet all day that dog stuck by Grandma. Everywhere. I thought it was like the fish on *Mutual of Omaha's Wild Kingdom,* the ones that live near the sharks as a means of survival. Then one day I was walking by the kitchen and I saw Grandma slipping the dog a piece of turkey. Very secretly. I thought I'd imagined it, so I told my brother, and he'd seen her slip something to the dog at dinner. Over the years the stories came out. Everyone in my family had witnessed Grandma secretly treating the dog.

Grandma gave out her love like she gave out that turkey. You had to pay attention or you'd miss it. But it was always there, never flagging, never in doubt. I never felt so safe as in that house.

I know the farm wasn't the life she'd wanted. She wanted to live in town. Sit in that stinky beauty shop or in the car all day on Main Street.

Every Christmas we gathered in the living room and Grandma sat down at the piano. With her high shaking voice, she sang old songs from the 1920s and 1930s. Even as the years progressed and her arthritis became unbearable, once a year she played through the pain, her piano sounding horribly out of tune until she burst into song and then it somehow all made sense.

To me, she truly was grace.

ACKNOWLEDGMENTS

THANK YOU TO EDITOR Ann Regan; working with her has been like an orange slice at mile twenty-two. To Pam McClanahan, director at Borealis Books, advisor, and wonderful editor of my first book. Thank you to my love and trusted first reader, Mary Ludington. To my mom, Dora; sister, Laura; brother, Steven; and the rest of the Kling/Dysart tree. To manager and godsend Mary McGeheran. To the folks at National Public Radio, especially Bob Boilen. To Tony Bol and Minnesota Public Radio. I'm grateful to the Seattle Repertory Theatre, the Guthrie Theater, the National Storytelling Festival, and to those who run the festivals, theaters, and gymnasiums where these stories lived before the page. To Steven Dietz, Ken Washington, David Esbjornson, Michael Sommers, Braden Abraham, Amy Poisson, Layne Kennedy, the Greilings, Mick Stephens, Tom Herberg, Mike Ericson, Aimee Bissonette, Greg Britton, Loren Niemi, Erin Sanders, Rob Simonds, Simone Perrin, Greg and Steve Myhr. To my teachers at Osseo and Gustavus Adolphus College.

AND, FINALLY, to my life-long mentor, the late Bill Holm.

Kevin Kling's Holiday Inn was designed and set in type by Percolator Graphic Design, Minneapolis. The type is Adobe Chaparral, designed by Carol Twombly. Printed by Maple Press, York, Pennsylvania.